SOMETHING FUNNY HAPPENED ON MY WAY TO THE ROSTRUM

by
D. Geoffrey Manton

SOMETHING FUNNY
HAPPENED ON MY WAY
TO THE ROSTRUM

by

D. GEOFFREY MANTON

To Maggie — with every good wish from the author
Geoff Manton

First Published 2001
© D. Geoffrey Manton 2001
ISBN 0 9515626 2 2

Edited by Harry Dagnall

Published by
Cavendish Philatelic Auctions Limited,
Cavendish House,
153-157 London Road, Derby DE1 2SY,
Great Britain.

Front cover illustration: Cartoon of a Cavendish auction by Bryan Hawkins.
Inside front cover illustration: Front cover of catalogue for Cavendish's first auction,
23rd January 1952.
Back cover illustration: Geoffrey Manton.
Inside back cover illustration: a selection of Cavendish catalogues, 1952-2001.

Printed by Scotia Press, Ann Street, Leicester, LE1 1SR, Great Britain

CONTENTS

FOREWORD

When it was suggested four years ago that I might care to put down some "recollections" for production in the "Chronicle" I expected that it would amount to two articles at the most. In fact they represent random memories covering a period of some 50 years now made more orderly by professional editing. They are confined generally, but not exclusively, to matters of a philatelic nature. Other memories have, of course, flooded in – family, social, sporting, travel – of not much interest to anybody but myself.

In the main my recollections centre around events connected with Cavendish and its history. I first met Frank Laycock at the Canadian Philatelic Society of G.B. Dinner at Harrogate in 1969. Eric Bielby who was the President that year had invited me to act as Auctioneer at that particular convention. This was an enjoyable occasion for myself and my wife, and I subsequently became a member of the Society and its Honorary Auctioneer. I would see Frank at most of the subsequent conventions and we became good friends.

In 1972 I had an offer from Stanley Gibbons. This was made at an early morning working breakfast at the Philatelic Congress of Great Britain which was being held at Llandudno that year. A.L. (Mick) Michael was the Chairman of Gibbons at that time and the general idea was that I should move to London to take charge of Gibbons Auctions which would be run in tandem with Cavendish, the latter to remain as a separate entity in Derby. We discussed this at length and the terms of my directorship over a period of some weeks, both in London and at Derby. Eventually we were unable to agree the final details of the proposal and the matter was ended amicably. In the circumstances it has been a decision I have never regretted, but in subsequent years I gave much thought to how I would eventually dispose of the company. I hoped that it would remain a family firm and would not have to join one of the London circuses. The matter was resolved for me in 1982 when a letter arrived from Frank Laycock. His family textile business had been sold and he thought he would like to "go into stamps". Eventually this resulted in him buying Cavendish, with me to stay on for a year – an arrangement which was extended during the whole of his ownership of the company. This period cemented our friendship and our common interests included shooting. On several occasions we would be guests at each other's shoots in Derbyshire and Yorkshire.

I had known the Grimwood-Taylor family since quite soon after my arrival in Derbyshire in 1947 through meeting at various Territorial Army functions. I can well remember James as a small boy being brought into the shop by his mother. He was a most exacting customer and I would hand him over to Sergius Matveiff, the Manager at that time, who possessed inexhaustible patience!! I did not see much of James during his time away at school and university but one day his father, Richard, 'phoned me and said "Geoffrey, a terrible thing has happened, James wants to become a stamp monger, what shall we do?" Well, who better to ask than another stamp monger! By now, of course, Cavendish was firmly established. James no longer had a keen interest in stamps as such – postal history was the thing. He spent a very short time with us before joining Argyll Etkin, the postal history specialists. This was well suited to his talents and he very soon made his mark.

Some six years after Frank Laycock acquired Cavendish he felt the urge to return to the Yorkshire Dales. It was fortuitous that at the same time James wanted to come home to Derbyshire. The result is now history, during which time the company has gone from strength to strength.

I remain as a consultant – not that anybody consults me very much these days, but it's all good fun. This then is a potted history of one period during the life of Cavendish Auctions.

The book must be dedicated to the loyal staff without whom my business could never have been built up from virtually nothing, and to the many friends in the stamp world who have made work such a pleasure.

I have been fortunate in having two wives, both much too good for me. Mary (my first wife who passed away some years ago) provided sterling support during 45 years of marriage, and Pamela who has cheerfully coped with my funny and often difficult ways, and who originally suggested that I write some sort of 'memoir'.

D G Manton

"He was a most exacting customer…" James Grimwood-Taylor in 1964, aged 7.

Surrounded by the Cavendish team in 1995.
Front row from left, John Cowell, James Grimwood-Taylor, Pat Grimwood-Taylor, myself,
Sonia Wroblewski, Ken Baker and Paul Grimwood-Taylor;
back row from left, Nick Wraith, Margaret Jones, Ian Kellock, Anne Perkins, Richard Farman
and Christine Woodcock.

INTRODUCTION

Philately should be a relaxing and enjoyable hobby; if it can be combined with humour, then the pleasure is all the greater. I have been uniquely fortunate to have encountered Geoff Manton at every stage of my philatelic 'career' – I have never yet had what my late father would have called a 'proper job' – and I hope that this slender volume will prove how lucky I have been.

Here is a series of recollections which bring to life the philatelic world during the decade before I was born, and record many significant collectors and philatelic events of my first forty years as a philatelist. Cavendish's 50th Birthday – 23rd January 2002 – seemed a great excuse to produce a permanent reminder of a man who has always combined philately with humour, as well as courtesy with vigour.

The reader who has not had the good fortune to hear Geoff Manton as raconteur or after-dinner speaker will gain some insight into his genius for this difficult art. Perhaps it will inspire others to try the same recipe. After all, philately is a hobby – it need not always be totally serious and should never be dull! Geoff inspired many a Derbyshire schoolboy to take up collecting, and I owe him a personal "thank you" both for being the catalyst that then enabled me to become a professional philatelist, and for creating 'Cavendish Auctions' to enable me to return to my native county and continue the traditions of the unique, collector-friendly business that he founded back in 1952.

Further *"Manton Recollections"* will be published in future issues of the quarterly *"Cavendish Chronicle"*, and I am glad to say that Geoff shows no sign of running out of suitable tales to tell. He and I would both like to thank the 'Cavendish Crew' in Derby for making all this possible, and to thank Harry Dagnall in particular for volunteering to act as Editor. The biggest "thank you" goes to all Cavendish's thousands of buyers and vendors, and complimentary copies of this book will be sent to all subscribers as at Christmas 2001 as a mark of our gratitude.

Geoffrey Manton in full flow (at the Canadian Philatelic Society of Great Britain conference in Chester in 1993).

James Grimwood-Taylor
Chairman
Cavendish Philatelic Auctions

CHAPTER 1

The Early Years

Having been afflicted with anecdotage for some years now my friends have suggested that I put some thoughts down on paper so that others may share their suffering.

It is certainly true that the memory of events fifty or more years ago seems clear, while that of more recent happenings is quick to fade.

Nevertheless the early days of Cavendish may be of interest – the sales which we held in the Midlands and the North – the characters we met and the friendships we made. In those very early days four-margined blacks made two pounds each and a 'useful general collection' (a description beloved by stamp auctioneers to this day) could be bought for five or six pounds.

However, let us start at the beginning. In the 1930s, and earlier, nearly all school boys, and probably very many girls, collected stamps. It tended to be seasonal, commencing in November after the 'conker' season, and would continue up to Easter.

I was born and spent all my early years in the Wirral. My father was 'in shipping' in Liverpool and I suppose I was about six (in 1927) when he started bringing stamps home from his office. Later he wrote and published a technical work on Ship Repairing which sold world-wide and the consequent correspondence became an excellent source of stamps. This then was my introduction to what was to become a life-long interest and occupation.

Stamps in Liverpool

My maternal grandmother lived in Weston-super-Mare and up to when I was about 14 a large part of my summer, Christmas and Easter holidays would be spent at her home. Other cousins would also be there. Some of my early stamp purchases were made from a stationer's shop which also dabbled in stamps. This I think must have been in the winter because the summer holidays offered other attractions – did the sun shine every day or is this just a figment of my imagination? I do remember for sure seeing my first county match, Somerset versus Sussex with the great Duleep Sinhji in action, and I have recently been able to confirm this by reference to Wisden. I remember one summer in particular when, in company with my cousin Pat, we would go every day to the Grand Pier. The attraction was one 'Dare Devil Peggy' who would remove his wooden leg and climb a ladder to a platform which appeared to us to be at an incredible height. Having arrived he would set his clothing on fire and dive into a large barrel of water emitting a blood-curdling scream. Perhaps the attraction was to see if he would one day miss the barrel! After this we would take ourselves to Forte's Ice Cream Parlour to enjoy a "North Pole" before lunch.

Lord Forte in his autobiography writes that his parents, who had a restaurant in Glasgow, sent him, as part of his training, to his Uncle in Weston, who owned the establishment. Who knows – perhaps Pat and I were served with our "North Poles" by the future Lord Forte!

Pat is six months older than I and was always the instigator of our various ploys. I regard her as my intellectual cousin. She lives in Arizona and I send her all the *'Daily Telegraph'* Crossword puzzles and some from *'The Times'*. She generally solves three or four a day. Small wonder that I always defer to her.

During the pre-Second World War years, and indeed from the turn of the century, Merseyside, and Liverpool in particular, was a hot bed of stamp collectors. Its position as a major seaport had much to do with this. It is not surprising that over the years this City spawned many dealers to cater for this situation. One of the early stamp dealers was Redpath who handled very many of the classic rarities and achieved a degree of fame in the stamp world.

1

From about the age of 14 I made regular visits to the Liverpool stamp shops during school holidays. It was then possible to buy a lot for a little, and as I had already set myself up as the school stamp dealer I sometimes had a pound or two to spend.

Sometimes I would travel by rail from West Kirby and through to Liverpool from Birkenhead on the 'underground', as it was known. However, by far the most enjoyable route was to cross the Mersey on the Seacombe or Birkenhead ferry. The waterway would be crowded with cargo steamers, Canadian Pacific liners and Cunarders. The Overhead Railway, running the length of the river frontage, afforded the sight of crowded dockyards and warehouses. Ship builders like Cammell Lairds on the Birkenhead side and ship repairing and fitting out companies mainly on the Liverpool side added to the activity – now largely gone thanks in large measures to Union pressures.

Moorfields, near Exchange Station, was the hub of the commercial philatelic scene. Mr. Sinclair-Brown was an up-market dealer who had little to offer the younger collector. A few doors away was Martin A. McGoff. He carried a very extensive and varied stock, appealing equally to the beginner and advanced collector. Round the corner from Moorfields, in Leather Lane, was Miss Darcy's shop. She was a very pleasant lady who always had time to spare for small boys. This was a regular port of call and I'm sure I came away with many bargains.

It was in an office above Miss Darcy's that Mr. Metcalfe started the Commonwealth Stamp Co., specialising in K.G.VI issues and publishing the well known catalogue of that name. In Cook Street was Stephen's Shop. The owner was seldom present but a helpful manageress attended to customers. I was told that Mr. Stephen (if that was his name) was employed by Imperial Airways and this would account for the specialisation in flown covers. It was here that I obtained my first Penny Black. It was concealed inside a packet of 100 Penny Reds which cost 1/6d – not a particularly cheap price at that time. I bought several of these 1d Red packets later but no more Blacks appeared. Perhaps I had stumbled across a 'loss leader'.

The firm of Lisburn and Townsend was in Islington. They will surely be remembered by all who had been young collectors between the wars. They were the best known of all the juvenile approval dealers and their advertisements, always offering a 'free gift', were in all the boys' magazines. One day, long after I had graduated from this stage of collecting, I found myself in Islington, an area not far from St. George's Hall in the centre of the City, and called on the firm. For some reason which escapes me I was shown into the Managing Director's office. To my complete surprise he was Mr. W. Cooper – he and his wife were friends of my parents and as far as I knew his occupation was not known to us. I spent an interesting hour being shown the working of this aspect of stamp dealing, including some 40 rather splendid young ladies busily mounting up approval sheets. When I later mentioned this to my mother she said "Willie Cooper always had an eye for the ladies".

Surely the most eccentric of the Liverpool dealers was Mr. Shaw on Brownlow Hill, where he combined stamps with antiquarian books. Victorian, Edwardian and George V high values were a speciality and these were displayed individually in small photo-frames on shelves between the books. Mr. Shaw always wore a schoolmaster's gown and sometimes a cap to match and when you entered the shop he would make a dramatic appearance as if from nowhere. It could be quite intimidating. He was bombed out during the raids on Liverpool but he re-opened in a small shop nearer the centre. I called there once during a short leave in, I think, late 1943, and found that he now presented a more normal appearance. He offered me a superb used G.B. George V £1 Green Block of four for £10. Sadly I could not run to this on a Second Lieutenant's eleven shillings a day. I have always remembered and regretted this.

During the 1930s two of the large department stores in Liverpool had stamp departments. There was a small one in Lewis's selling ready priced material and publications. The one in the basement at George Henry Lee's was a much more ambitious affair and was run like a normal stamp dealer's shop. It was here that I bought the nucleus for a collection of Chile which occupied me on and off for many years.

Messrs. G.P. Vessey, the one-time Whitstable Auctioneers, used to hold occasional sales in the North and would visit Liverpool once or twice a year. When I was 14, or probably 15, I attended one of these sales at, I think, the Angel Hotel. As this was a 'first' for me I can remember the day quite well. I had only 10/- to spend and bought a Falklands lot (consisting of two complete sheets of each of the $\frac{1}{2}$d and 1d War stamps) for six shillings, later securing a pair of early Peruvian items for 3/6d – yes you could buy lots at these prices in those days. At the end of the sale a gentleman approached me and said he had meant to bid on the Peru and would I accept 5/-, which I did. To complete my day when I got home I found that instead of two sheets each of the Falklands there were in fact four sheets of each. I'm sure that it was this day's experience that persuaded me that there was 'money in stamps' and that a stamp dealer's life was the life for me.

I was always a little envious of Gordon Sowerbutts. He was two or three years older than I and had persuaded his father to let him leave school early and open a stamp shop in Water Street. His father was, I think, a fruit importer and the shop was in the basement of his offices and I spent many a happy and instructive hour there.

In many of the offices in this business quarter of Liverpool the stamps on incoming mail were an office boy's perk. Around one o'clock there would be a small queue of these chaps bringing that morning's haul for sale. I seem to remember there would often be many Spanish Civil War stamps, all torn from the envelopes – sadly Postal History was not a thing that mattered very much in those days.

The War Years

1946 Officers P.T. Course at Aldershot. I am second from the right in the back row. Also in the photograph (front row, second from right) is Billy Wright, later to become Captain of the English soccer team, here as one of the four instructors.

All this pleasurable philatelic activity came to an abrupt halt at the end of August, 1939. Many of us had joined the Territorials during our last year at school – no questions were asked! Gordon's shop closed and he was away to join, I think, the Liverpool Scottish. I was destined for our local Royal Horse Artillery – phase one of my stamp activity was at an end.

Although the war years halted any real philatelic activity one very occasionally met and talked with a fellow collector in the Forces. This was about as far as things went. For a time I carried in my kit an S.G. Miniature album. I thought perhaps that a small country like Iceland might be both easy to achieve and the stamps cheap whenever I might come across a dealer during my travels – how wrong can you be! In the event the collection got nowhere. This was just as well because all my kit, including the miniature album, was stolen during the lengthy time spent in a Military Hospital having foolishly got myself accidentally shot.

The stamp trade has always been rich in 'characters'. One such character was Sydney Homsy, who may possibly be remembered by older collectors. Homsy occupied a small third floor office off the Strand, near to Aldwych Underground Station. During 1940/41 I sometimes had the odd twenty-four hours' leave in London and on two or three occasions called on him. He was an extremely large man and as far as I could tell never moved from behind his equally large desk. I remember wondering if he slept there! On his left and right two saucepans boiled continually, one to provide a constant supply of coffee, the other to soak stamps off paper, another non-stop activity. The last time I visited Sydney was the morning following a heavy air-raid. The streets were full of broken glass, rubble and fire hoses. The office building was standing but certainly the worse for wear, and appeared to be unoccupied. Not so – Sydney Homsy in his usual urbane manner was seemingly unperturbed by the water which was cascading through the ceiling a few yards away and disappearing through the floor. I felt sure he had been there all night.

A characteristic Homsy advertisement, from *'Stamp Collecting'* 1926.

I have mentioned Sydney Homsy but many other dealers, large and small, survived the 'blitz'. Many evacuated to the country together with their stocks, but others soldiered on in London. The Chancery Lane Safe Deposit contained many valuable stamp stocks which were damaged by water and which appeared on the market after the war. I suspect that much of the re-gummed early material, which is so often offered, results from this wartime catastrophe.

During my time in Perth (where I was posted in 1946) it became a habit on Saturdays to call at the Station Hotel for a drink before lunch. On one such Saturday I found the bar full of strangers and the barman told me that they were stamp collectors *"or some such thing, funny lot, but they know how to drink"*. I discovered that it was the inaugural meeting of the Canadian Philatelic Society of Great Britain; little did I know that 18 years later I would become the Honorary Auctioneer of this very friendly society and have the honour of proposing the toast to the ladies at the 50th Anniversary Dinner. Although I don't myself collect Canada I can truly say that membership over the years has given me intense pleasure. Every collector of British North America stamps and postal history should become a member. There are regional branches, a bi-monthly magazine, exchange packets, a superb lending library and every year a four day convention with splendid displays, interesting outings and, of course, the opportunity to renew friendships – so enjoyable are these occasions that several of our Canadian members come to England year after year.

The quietest New Year I have spent was, strangely enough, that in Scotland in 1946/47. Highland District H.Q. was in Perth and I had somehow persuaded higher authority that for various reasons it would be advantageous if I lived out of mess in a private hotel.

Looking back it was certainly to my advantage! It was pointed out to me that on occasions when I was Duty Officer, about once a month, I would be required to be in mess. It seemed a good deal! It was decreed that I should be Duty Officer at New Year, which was fair enough – I was a member of the only English regiment in the H.Q. The mess was at Bridge of Earn, outside Perth, in a high castle-like pile, which had been requisitioned from one of the Highland aristocrats. His name escapes me except that he was "of that ilk", whatever that may mean. I reported the day before and it was suggested that I read the standing orders for coping with any emergency that might occur in the command, which covered all the areas north of the Clyde and Forth, including the Orkneys. The Argylls were at Stirling Castle, the Camerons at Inverness, The Gordons at Aberdeen, The Seaforth Highlanders at Fort George and The Black Watch at Perth.

At Elgin we had a large Infantry Training Centre and there were, of course, smaller establishments all over the area. By lunchtime everyone from the General downwards had departed and for the next three days Highland District was virtually commanded by a junior officer – and an English one at that! In the event I did not receive a single telephone call or alarm. It was as though the entire army had closed down and gone home for Hogmanay – which was probably the case.

My only companions in the mess were German Prisoners who looked after me extremely well. Dinner on New Year's Eve was an unforgettable affair. The dining room was vast and dominated by a huge table where I sat in solitary state. A magnificent log fire was the only cheerful sight. The Mess Sergeant stood behind me throughout the meal and two other prisoners brought in the various courses. There was much clicking of heels but no conversation. At 12 o'clock I invited the Sergeant to join me in a glass of brandy. He politely refused with more heel clicking, obviously considering that this would be improper! So ended my quietest and indeed oddest New Year's Eve.

The only connection the foregoing narrative has with stamps and postal history is that during the weekend I had ample time to sort out some material I had recently bought at a sale in Edinburgh. Occasional sales were held in Glasgow, Dundee and Edinburgh by local auctioneers. They were ready-made sales which were supplied by a Scottish dealer named Hislop, and which ceased upon his untimely death during the 1950s. Mr. Hislop would make regular forays up to London and attend several stamp auctions until he had been able to purchase enough material to re-lot for his sales in Scotland. These were the days before philatelic auctioneers published estimated values in their catalogues, and because of this there was very little competition from postal buyers. It was possible for dealers to purchase large lots at London sales, then break them down to re-sell at a worthwhile profit.

I myself had an early experience of this. A prominent local collector had died shortly after I had started Cavendish Auctions in 1952. I had hoped that we would be entrusted with the sale of his extensive and valuable collections. The solicitor handling the estate thought otherwise and it was sent up to London for disposal. I attended the sale. The collection was sold in large country lots, no attempt having been made to break them up, and I was able to purchase about half of the material on offer. When re-lotted it realised rather more than twice the purchase price.

It was in 1946/7 that I began to think seriously of making a career in stamps. At the time I was on General Barber's staff at Highland District H.Q. in Perth. This was a very happy year for me, and I did not suffer from being a member of the only English Regiment in the H.Q! Small stamp auctions took place in Dundee and Edinburgh and I had ample time to attend these. I made a number of stamp friends including the late Harry Ireland, who was an accomplished artist and was at that time art-editor on the 'Scottish Field'. He had a formidable British Colonial collection which was eventually sold by Cavendish. Another friend was Jack Henderson, and also his parents. Jack's Stamp and Antique Shop in Perth is today a mecca for collectors in that part of Scotland.

INTER-SERVICES ATHLETIC CHAMPIONSHIPS, 1946 ARMY TEAM.
I was here at the height of my athletic career (seated third from the left in the second row).

CHAPTER 2

The Birth of Cavendish

Derby Gets a New Stamp Shop

On the 1st September 1947 I became a civilian again. My wife Mary and I had agreed that stamp dealing would be given a twelve month trial and that hopefully we would still be eating at the end of that period. We had bought a minute cottage near Matlock. Neither of us had any roots in Derbyshire or, indeed, had ever visited the county, and I have often been asked why we settled here. It was quite by chance. During the previous two years I had discovered that I still retained something of my pre-war talent for athletics. During July 1947 I was en route for the Army Championships at Aldershot and we stopped off at Chesterfield which was the venue for the Northern Counties Championships. Afterwards, having two or three days to kill, we went by bus to Matlock which we were told was a beauty spot not to be missed. This then is how we found the cottage and came to live in Derbyshire. On the 1st October a very small stamp shop opened for business in Derby – the first day's takings were two pence, not an entirely auspicious start. In all enterprises an element of luck is needed and I think we had our share, especially by settling in this part of the country.

The shop, or rather a third floor office, which opened in Derby in 1947 made steady, albeit modest, progress. In the general absence of television the "school-boy" trade continued to prosper for a few years. On Saturday mornings in particular the staircase to our office was filled with a lively lot of young collectors, often to the irritation of our neighbours.

It was not long before I acquired my first assistant. He was "Wiggy" Taylor who had just retired from Rolls-Royce. Our hobby abounds with "characters" who may be found on both sides of the counter. "Wiggy" was certainly one of these and I remember him with much affection. He originated from Manchester and had been a lifelong collector. He had two wigs, one so decrepit that it was itself bald, and he always wore a cap in addition, both in and out of the office. The other was a rather splendid example reserved for Sunday use and for the annual visit to Blackpool. He also owned a camera which was surely a collector's piece. Each year he would disappear beneath a black cloth to take a single photograph of his wife and daughter – always in the same position on the promenade.

Sorting new issues in the shop, 1956.

7

His forte was soaking, cataloguing and mounting stamps, and he also looked after any young collectors who came in. On one occasion I overheard the following conversation when the customer was taking an age to make his selection:

Wiggy -   *"What do you collect then?"*
Boy   -   *"Famous men."*
Wiggy -   *"How much do you want to spend"?*
Boy   -   *"A Penny."*

And Wiggy replied with the immortal words:

"You'll get no famous men for a penny."

Wiggy had been employed as store-man by Henry Royce who was then manufacturing cranes in Manchester. He obviously thought a lot of young Taylor because on his departure to Derby to join forces with the Hon. Rolls he gave him much of the contents of his office. He also promised to send for him when he had an opening, and this he duly did. When Wiggy died he left me Royce's office chair which I used until quite recently. It has now gone to Peter Brack who, as well as being an authority on the stamps of many Latin American countries, is also an avid collector of Rolls-Royce memorabilia.

One of our earliest customers was the Rev. James Compton-Bracebridge, Rector of Morley, near Derby. He became a close friend and every Wednesday he would come into Derby with his gardener, one "Pop" Seal. While "Pop" did the family shopping James and I would adjourn, firstly to the "Buck in the Park", adjacent to our premises, and then to the "Old Bell" in Sadlergate where "Pop" would join us and we would enjoy a fairly liquid lunch. James loved to shock people, especially when wearing his customary clerical garb, but he was a true Christian and generous to a fault, supporting many charities. He was a cricket enthusiast and would attend all the Test Matches at Trent Bridge and Edgbaston. Once, en route for a Test at Edgbaston, we stopped to take refreshment at Lichfield. Here we fell in with a group of farmers, it being market day. The result of this was that we arrived at the ground after tea in time to see the last three overs of the day. It was deemed politic that we should both return home with final score cards so we retired to the Beer Tent to await them. It was here that a somewhat inebriated Irishman, apparently attracted by the "dog collar", approached James and asked him the difference between Low Church and High Church. Without hesitation, James replied *"High Church drink – Low Church eat."*

An earlier member of the Bracebridge family was Selina, the friend and companion of Florence Nightingale, and the family possessed much Nightingale memorabilia. I was given a letter addressed to Florence at the Military Hospital, Scutari, which encouraged me to make a small collection of Crimea War material. James himself had a fairly extensive general collection. He was not a philatelist in the true sense but enjoyed his stamps and all the fun which went with them. He lived to nearly 100 and after his wife died he retired to the "Home of St. Barnabas" near Tunbridge Wells. My wife and I visited him there on one occasion and found that, although the accommodation was very comfortable, the preponderance of bishops and senior clergy depressed him!

It is well remarked that appearance can be deceptive. One day an oldish gentleman came into the office. He wore bicycle clips and was rather shabbily dressed, and asked if we had any good stamps for sale. A Sierra Leone Wilberforce set was on view at the time at about £40. I indicated this and he said *"keep it for me; here is £20 on account"*. *"See if you can find anything better for next week"*. He remained a considerable buyer for many years, cycling from Leicester about every three weeks, and was interested only in complete sets of top quality which he held for investment. Many years later Cavendish had the sale of this holding.

Over the years Derby has had many prominent philatelists, including several Fellows of the Royal, together with one Vice-President and one President. Derby Philatelic Society dates from 1905 and during the 1950s and 1960s the doyen was the late W.H. Miles-Marsden, FRPSL. He was a lawyer in the city and prominent in many fields. He was one of the last big general collectors and his albums covered a world-wide range. He had no time for covers – the stamp was the thing, a view which he would put forcefully on occasion. His one speciality was Bosnia, comprising many albums, which I confess I found pretty boring. He also called his house 'Bosnia'. When he died I had the task of selling the collections to a New York philatelist, the only other collector of Bosnia of similar calibre. It had previously been agreed between them that the survivor would purchase the collection of the deceased.

Every season Miles-Marsden would display one of his collections to the Society and I remember the time when the subject was Virgin Islands. At question time one of the new members had the temerity to ask why all the stamps were mint. The great man looked at him sternly and replied *"Young man – you should know that used virgins are hard to find"*. Over the years some of the most important collections have been displayed before the Derby Society. On one occasion I remember meeting the late H.V. Adams from the London train. He was carrying his Grand Prix G.B. Collections in two large butcher's paper carriers. He explained that this was by far the safest mode of transportation.

As 1950 approached, D.G. Manton Limited, or Derbyshire Stamps as we became known, was becoming quite well known in the Midlands and extra help, both full and part time, was taken on. I always deplored having to work on Saturdays and without doubt my family suffered, although uncomplainingly. It was however a necessity because this was the day when so many customers came from Nottingham, Leicester, the Potteries and even from as far afield as Birmingham and Sheffield.

During weekdays we would often see collectors from the South and other parts of England, who were in the city on business, and many of them became regular visitors. I still made my bi-weekly visits to the London sales and by this means managed to acquire an ever changing stock. In the early days callers from overseas often had currency problems and it was sometimes possible to agree a barter transaction. I remember John Vandenburg, a bulb grower from Haarlem, who sent me the finest box of tulips I could possibly hope for. Then again, one of the West Indian cricketers, when over here, swapped me one of his old bats for stamps. To this day I regret it being used for beach cricket during two Cornish holidays and finally disintegrating.

My first advertisement for the auctions, *'Stamp Collecting'*, November 9th, 1951.

Thematic collecting was in its infancy during the period I describe. It is now, of course, a very firmly established field of stamp collecting, but has never really appealed to me, although I admire the expertise shown at exhibitions. I remember one gentleman, who collected camels on stamps, who would visit the shop most Saturdays in search of these creatures. Beyond offering the ubiquitous Camel postman I was never able to help and began to feel pretty hopeless as a stamp dealer. One Saturday I had chanced upon what I felt would fit the bill. It was from South America I think and I produced it with a flourish. He studied it long and hard and finally said *"That's not a Camel. That's a Dromedary – I don't collect Dromedaries"*. I think it was this that finally decided me to quit stamp dealing and move into the Auction field. This then was the probable start of Cavendish Auctions.

The front of my shop, c.1953.

I Ascend the Rostrum

During the latter half of 1951 I began to think seriously of setting up an Auction business. At that time stamp auctions were virtually unknown in the Midlands and the North. Vessey would come to Liverpool or Manchester about once a year, and the occasional itinerant auctioneer would make a rare appearance. My thinking was that regular auctions, held in most of the major towns and cities, would attract buyers who hitherto had little choice beyond travelling up to London sales. It is true, of course, that bidding by post was a possibility. However, it was only during the previous few years that auction catalogues had started to print valuations as a guide, and so the habit of postal bidding was slow to start.

I am often asked "why Cavendish"? The reason was that during our first year the sales were administered from Cavendish House in Chesterfield. The late Helen Cavendish, Aunt of the Duke of Devonshire, was an early customer. She once asked me why we used her family name but she readily agreed that it was far better than Cavendish Motors, Cavendish Laundry etc., there being many such firms in Derbyshire!

Our first few sales were modest affairs, and from the beginning the problem was not that of sufficient buyers, but of attracting enough vendors with material of the right calibre. We were really pioneers in our field and during the first few years sales were held in Derby, Chesterfield, Nottingham, Sheffield, Hanley, Stafford, Manchester, Buxton, Leeds, Wakefield, Doncaster, Rotherham, Birmingham, Oxford, Leicester, Loughborough, Coventry and Bradford.

Gradually the number of venues was narrowed down to those where the support was greatest and eventually Derby, Manchester and Leeds became the favoured towns. We had, however, gained a following in all the places we had visited and many collectors were prepared to travel to our sales elsewhere.

The early sales generated a club-like atmosphere as collectors from various parts would meet each other, initially at three-weekly intervals, and later every month. Stamp collectors generally are gregarious creatures and the various hotel bars were well patronised both before and after the sale. As I was usually able to join a congenial group at the end of the proceedings my circle of friends widened. With one or two exceptions we have in our archives all the sale catalogues we have produced during the last 50 years.

A roomful of buyers at our November 1962 auction in Manchester.

The first sale was held at the Railway Institute in Derby on the 23rd January 1952. I remember well my début as a stamp auctioneer - the previous night I had held a rehearsal in the dining room at home with members of my family! At the inaugural sale the local Philatelic Society attended in force together with a number of collectors from further afield, and some non-collectors who were curious to know what it was all about. The catalogue reveals that we were offering 303 lots, the highest valuations being £42 each for collections of Ceylon and Egypt. The many G.B. lots included several 4-margin Penny Blacks at 30/- a time, while the 1840 2d Blues were valued at 75/-. One Edward VII £1 superb used was 55/- and the 1913 £1 Green in similar condition was valued at £7. These were the prices ruling fifty years ago. [See Appendix for a reproduction of part of this first ever "Cavendish" catalogue].

The result of the sale was moderately successful, sufficiently so to encourage me to continue with the enterprise, although one punter on leaving was heard to remark *"He'll have to do better than that"*! This was in fact the late Frank Peach who later became a good friend. Frank was a formidable philatelist who formed several specialised collections in various fields. These we sold two or three years ago. His other great interest was cricket and he was for many years chairman of the Derbyshire County Cricket Supporters' Club which was responsible for raising considerable sums for Derbyshire C.C.C. When he died we discovered that he also had an exceptional collection of cricket memorabilia which we also sold. It realised quite astonishing prices.

Frank Peach

During the first couple of years of sales the lots could be contained in about three large suitcases. These could just be accommodated in my first car after the war, a 1932 Wolsley Hornet Special, Reg. AGP99, which I bought for £170. I was assured by the vendor that it had been raced at Brooklands and Brands Hatch, and certainly when it was in good form nothing on the road could touch it. The six cylinders were grouped in pairs and it had the alarming habit of blowing between two cylinders. I was the last person who should have owned such a car as I am completely unmechanically minded and I think every garage man between Matlock and Derby helped to keep it on the road.

Once, returning from holiday in Cornwall, I had to seek assistance from a garage in Barnstaple. When I went to collect it the rather elderly mechanic said *"Very sporty m'dear"*; *"Yes"* I replied proudly; *"I shouldn't be too sporty m'dear"* he said *"I don't like the look of that back axle"*. The end came one day when it was moving like the proverbial bomb and it suddenly blew up. However, it never let me down when travelling to or from a sale and I still remember it with affection.

For quite a few years the auctions were run in tandem with and indeed were a minor appendage to the retail business in Derby. Eventually, of course Cavendish Auctions grew considerably and Derbyshire Stamps had to go. I owe so much to the help I received from my late wife Mary. She really knew nothing about stamps, and did not want to, but on sale days she would travel into Derby and take care of the shop. Of course much of the stock was unpriced but this would not deter her. She would ask the potential buyer what he thought he ought to pay! As far as I know she was never let down - such was her personality and popularity. Later on she attended all the sales when she would look after the visitors' book and made many friends. On occasions she was obliged to act as cashier. Handling money, giving change and computing V.A.T. were not her strong points but this was no handicap. I think she used the same methods as in the shop!

Inevitably as the sales grew the party atmosphere which was such a feature in the early sales grew less, although the good humour which attended even the most important of sales was always present. As this book reveals, the characters, both buyers and vendors, have always been with us, and it is this which has made my business life such a pleasure.

Expansion

Looking through over 600 past catalogues is a fascinating exercise in that it refreshes the mind and the memory of events and people of so many years ago. By the early 1960s we had become well established in the Midlands and the North and also had very many buyers in other parts of Britain and overseas. During this time we were joined by Sheila Kimber and Geoffrey Whitehead. We had advertised for a lady with a sense of humour and Sheila certainly needed that. On arrival she thought very little of our office procedures and she set about re-organising these without delay. Geoff. quickly became our chief describer and his encyclopaedic memory was often to prove of inestimable value to the firm. Both stayed with me until I sold the company, and beyond, and I owe much to them for their expertise and friendship.

John Parkin proposing me as a Fellow of the Canadian Philatelic Society.

As time went by they were joined by, among others, the late Joyce Robinson, a character with diverse talents, and also by Marjorie Eggleton and John Parkin. They all made important contributions to Cavendish and are happily remembered, not only by me but also by so many of our buyers who came into contact with them. The late Fred Lineham and the late Harry Calvert will also be remembered from our early sales when they helped for the sheer love of it. By 1963 we were beginning to attract many "name" collections for sale. That year we offered the "Harry Ireland" Colonies collection and the "Tomlinson" World Wide mint collections. The latter was an extraordinary offering which came in two trunks with everything still in the transparent envelopes as purchased. The value was considerable and the collection was dispersed over a number of sales. I well remember taking delivery of this property. Having spent several hours making a preliminary valuation I was about to depart at about 11 p.m. when the vendor said I could not go yet as *"I go on the air at midnight"*. He was of course a Radio "Ham" and after a drink and some sandwiches we proceeded to another part of the house which was fitted up with what was obviously much sophisticated radio equipment.

On the stroke of twelve he sent out his call sign and commenced a dialogue with fellow "Hams" in various parts of the world. He told me this would go on until about 4 a.m. but I got away after about an hour. It was before the motorways had reached the North of England and I was faced with a two hours' drive. My wife was with me on this occasion; she seldom complained but sometimes asked *"couldn't I think of an easier way to make a living"?*

A regular attender at our sales in Leeds and Manchester during the late 1950s and early 1960s was Eric Green of Bradford. A larger than life figure, he is remembered well by many of our buyers who attended those early sales. Eric was a very big man with a large heart and an enviable thirst. He had spent most of his life in South Africa, returning to Yorkshire soon after the second world war. He seldom bothered to view lots, but would mark up his catalogue before the sale and on arrival would sign in before adjourning to the bar, not to reappear until the sale commenced at two o'clock when in those days the bar was, perhaps fortunately, obliged to close. At about four o'clock the Head Porter would appear bearing him a tray with cup, saucer and large tea-pot. Few people realised that the tea-pot contained beer! Eric was a great patriot and collected only fine Colonials up to the end of George V reign. His method of collecting was somewhat unusual in that he had four sets of Imperial albums which he gradually filled, and thus required four of everything. He also had a more specialised collection of Cape Triangulars. He was indeed God's gift to auctioneers, and if bidding was flagging one would call out *"do you want this one Mr.Green"* and he invariably replied *"yes, I'll have the bugger"!* Eric did not drive, and after the Leeds sales we would take him home to Bradford where Effie, his minute and charming wife, would provide coffee and sandwiches.

At the conclusion of the sales in Manchester we would put him on the Bradford train in charge of the guard. Eric died during the summer of 1964 after a full life which included having been wounded on the Somme, a long love affair with Effie and, of course, his stamp collection. In due course we were privileged to sell his stamps in a series of sales.

In December 1964 we held our last sale in Birmingham and October 1966 was the last time we visited Sheffield. For the next ten years we confined our venues to Manchester, Leeds and occasionally Derby itself. I particularly recall the last sale at the Grand Hotel in Birmingham. I had sold the first few lots when a familiar figure entered the room. He appeared pre-occupied as he walked down the centre aisle and sat down in one of the front seats where he opened his brief case and took out a sheaf of papers – it was Enoch Powell, then M.P. for Wolverhampton. The sale continued, and looking slightly puzzled he re-packed his papers and departed as silently as he had arrived. There was, of course, a political meeting elsewhere in the hotel!

Many older collectors will remember Plymouth Philatelic Auctions. In its heyday (1955-65) it was very prominent in the provincial field, and we regarded it as our principal, but friendly, competitor. The owner was John Gilbert, himself a very colourful character His forte was writing amusing catalogue descriptions and compelling advertising copy. The drawings I have used on page 14 are from a calendar he produced in 1964. I always felt that his true calling should have been in the advertising field, or possibly as a newspaper columnist. Plymouth Auctions went into liquidation in 1966 and we were able to acquire the assets from the liquidator, of which the most important was the mailing list. This was very extensive and, largely because of the company's considerable expenditure on overseas advertising, included very many buyers from countries throughout the world. This

Busy viewing before a sale at the Queens Hotel, Manchester in 1962.

indeed became the nucleus of our world-wide connections of buyers and vendors. In the course of my negotiations with the liquidator, it transpired that the company also held the properties of over 200 vendors. I was able to convince him that this was purely material held in trust by Plymouth Auctions pending sale. We were able to rescue this material and take it back with us to Derby. Subsequently all but, I think, two of the vendors instructed us to sell in future sales and, as a result, we gained a few more regular vendors. The whole exercise proved ultimately well worthwhile. A personal spin-off for me was that John resigned from the office of Honorary Auctioneer of the Canadian Philatelic Society of Great Britain. The President that year was Eric Bielby, a friend and customer of Cavendish. He invited me to take over as Hon. Auctioneer and this has resulted in over thirty years of happy association with this splendid society.

Bishopmark

MARCH

Surcharge

APRIL

Imprint Block

MAY

Tete Beche

JUNE

Miniature Sheet

JULY

Complete Set

NOVEMBER

Some of the P.P.A. 1964 Calendar Cartoons

On the 9th December 1967 we held our first sale in our new saleroom in the Wardwick, Derby. Conveniently a small shoe warehouse in the same building as our offices near the city centre became vacant and we were able to acquire the lease. The conversion to a saleroom was not perfect, but it served us well for several years. The official opening was conducted by W.R. (Bill) Townsend, at that time President of the Royal Philatelic Society, London and was attended by the Mayor of Derby and many well-known members of the stamp fraternity. I cannot say that all went smoothly because from the start we were plagued by trouble with the new burglar alarm system, and hardly a night passed without Geoff. Whitehead, who was the main Derby keyholder, being called out. Somehow he retained his sanity.

Entertaining Bill Townsend when he opened Cavendish's first auction rooms in December 1967.

About this time I was in hospital for several weeks following major surgery. The sales continued, thanks to a dedicated staff and the help of good friends. Stewart Smith, an authority on Belgian Congo, emerged not only as an industrial chemist but also as a born auctioneer!

In March and April 1968 we held the "Corin" sales. This was an extensive general collection and Paul Corin was unusual in that he was the owner of an Organ Museum in the Tamar Valley. This was a commercial enterprise, comprising a large collection of continental organs, many specially brought over from Belgium. They were all housed in a disused mill and worked by compressed air connected to electric motors. He was clearly more interested in his organs than his stamp collection, the sale of which was to finance the import of further models. I travelled to Devon and we then spent several hours during which he demonstrated the organs before we loaded up the stamp albums and departed. Sadly Paul died soon after the stamps were sold and I do not know what happened to the Museum.

Cavendish Grows Up

To return to business matters, the 1970s were an interesting period for Cavendish. Refreshing the memory by looking through catalogues of sales at that time I can remember so many events and people both serious and laughable.

In October 1969 we held our 200th sale. As far as I can recall, it was a fairly normal type of sale. I do, however, remember that it was the first appearance of a farmer from a small village south of Buxton in the Peak District. When the sale began he seated himself immediately below the rostrum with his back to the auctioneer and placed his bids by scratching the back of his head. This was a little disconcerting but I soon got used to it. When I discussed this unusual practice with him after the sale, he said that not only was he able to watch the other bidders, but he was also able to conceal his own actions from them. He had found this method effective at cattle sales all his life! We had him for many seasons until his death about fourteen years ago.

In 1971 we had the Postal Strike which lasted for several weeks and we had to use some ingenuity to deliver both catalogues and the spoils to successful bidders. In many parts of the country we were able to organise delivery by hand, and on more than one occasion we arranged for catalogues for overseas clients to be posted in Germany or Holland.

During this time my wife Mary was staying with friends in India. She travelled all over the country and was away for over two months. We were, of course, unable to correspond but happily our friends made it possible for us to send and receive messages through the Head Office of Brooke-Bonds in London. Once someone 'phoned, *"I'm just back from India and your wife has asked me to tell you that she is in good form."* He added, *"At this time of the year there are a lot of parties in Calcutta - and your wife is usually there!"* This was no surprise to me!

It was about this time that we sold the Annetts stock. The advertisements of Anthony J. Annetts of Oxfordshire will be familiar to the older generation of collectors. He was an amiable eccentric who would bid, always by post, at nearly every stamp auction in the country. He favoured large lots, both miscellaneous and single country. These he would break up and offer in his advertisements. Often his purchases were so considerable and bulky that we would drive down to Sandford St. Martin and deliver in person. It was a rather rambling old house with an extensive garden which, although he collected a vast array of grass cutting machinery, was always overgrown. His pride and joy was a Rolls-Royce, which was used solely for a weekly visit to the village post-office and for taking his wife to the Women's Institute. It was also used for the annual expedition to Bognor, a two-day journey each way!

Visits to Anthony were full of incident, commencing by trying to survive the attack of a posse of savage Jack Russell terriers. Once I arrived by appointment at three in the afternoon and the place seemed deserted except for the maddened dogs hurling themselves at the door. Eventually Anthony appeared at an upstairs window in his pyjamas, having forgotten our arrangement! By Anthony's early death the stamp trade lost an unusual and loveable character.

In May 1971 came the sale of the Sir George Williamson collections of Canada, comprising both postal history and adhesives. This was the first occasion when we produced a catalogue with illustrations in colour. The sale attracted intense interest from collectors at home and in North America.

When I look through some of our sales catalogues of this period, I wonder where some of the lots we sold are today. There was the 1972 sale of Military Mail which included a letter from a father to his son in a Scottish Regiment advising him not to purchase a captaincy in Major Smithies' Regiment of Corsican Irregulars! In 1973 we sold a range of covers and cards from Sgt/Observer Booth believed to be the first British P.O.W. shot down on September 4th, 1939. Also in 1973 the auction took place of the experimental flights of the R100 and R101 in 1929/30 - a range of covers signed by the designer Barnes N. Wallis of Dambuster fame.

On the recommendation of Eric Green we held a couple of sales in Bradford. I remember him saying that in Bradford there were more cigars smoked per head of population than anywhere else in the country. This may have been a good reason for selling cigars but did not, in the event, prove a recommendation for selling stamps! One of these sales was at the Mechanics Institute, a large archaic building on three, possibly four, floors in the centre of the city. It has probably been swept away in the fullness of time and replaced by a supermarket or multi-storey car-park! From memory the sale took place on the third floor which was serviced by a large lift apparently operated by a system of counterweights or hydraulics. Just before the sale began, when it contained the entire Manchester contingent of buyers, it became stuck between two floors and, it being Saturday afternoon, an engineer could not be found for some two hours or more. However the sale had to go on and we were obliged to organise a relay system of runners between the sale room and the lift - it slowed up the proceedings but it worked! Sadly, a few days later one of the victims suffered a heart attack and died. He was not noticeably of a nervous disposition but I wondered if he had been affected by his enforced incarceration!

Many of our Yorkshire buyers will remember the sale held in the Crown Court at Leeds Town Hall. There was great competition to occupy the dock, while the auctioneer performed from the judge's seat. This was on the occasion of the Yorkshire Federation Convention.

During the 1960s and 70s we handled many fine properties which if sold today would make some remarkable prices. At that time I would usually go myself to take delivery of the material. This I enjoyed and had the pleasure of meeting many unusual and often delightful people. On one such occasion I went to see an eldery gentleman who was a retired schoolmaster very much of that rare breed, whom I shall call "Mr Chips". He resided in a one-time vicarage in Derbyshire surrounded by a large garden where, on arrival, I was met by his wife. She said that he was contemplating the sale of his collection and she hoped he would! She also said that if he looked like changing his mind I should bring up the subject of cricket!

Sheila Kimber, Geoff Whitehead and myself at the auction bench, Crown Court, Leeds Town Hall, May 1970.

"Mr Chips" proved to be a lovely man and stamps ranked second in his collecting interests. Books were his main love and his library occupied two of the downstairs rooms. He also collected old theatre posters, coins and indeed countless other fascinating objects including cricket memorabilia. No wonder his wife thought the time had come for a cull! I remember the stamp collection was general but with particular strength in G.B. and the United States – today it would be considered something special. The more we turned over the pages the more he felt disinclined to part with it; the time came for me to play my trump card – what did he think about the current Test Match series?

I can recall today that the West Indies were over here and Messrs. Ramadin and Valentine were creating havoc among the English batsmen. "Mr Chips" rose to his feet and said *"Follow me"*. From the hall-stand he handed me an old Gunn and Moore bat and led the way through the house. In the walled garden at the rear was a wicket and nets, obviously well used. For the next five or ten minutes he tied me up with slow-leg breaks before saying *"Right, let's go back and talk stamps"*. It was no surprise to me to hear some time later that one of his daughters was being considered for inclusion in the English Ladies Test Team to tour Australia.

While on the subject of cricket I can remember going to the Test Match at Trent Bridge that year. Behind us in the stand was an American who was being regaled by his host with the finer points of the English summer game. The play was particularly slow and, like all Americans, he was extremely polite but obviously bored by the whole proceedings. Suddenly a ripple of applause sounded around the ground:

The American	-	*"Say, what's that for?"*
His host	-	*"He's just bowled a maiden over"*.
The American	-	*"Well, wadaya know!"*

Another cricket anecdote comes to mind. In 1946 I was at Carlisle Castle. Leary Constantine was over with his West Indian Charity Eleven playing matches all over the country. On this day they were playing a Carlisle and District side on the Edenside ground below the Castle walls. The ground was full of spectators all looking forward to seeing Constantine play another of his entertaining innings. The great man came in at number three and he despatched the first ball with a prodigious hit to the boundary where he was caught! The cheer collapsed into a groan and there was silence for probably half a minute – then the umpire with great presence of mind shouted *"NO BALL"*

A New Home

For many years we had been seeking more suitable premises in the centre of Derby. Eventually, these were found for us by Trevor Clarke, a customer and friend of many years standing. Trevor, a surveyor and estate agent with a substantial business in Derby from which he has now retired, will be remembered for the splendid specialised collection of mint GB Edward VII issues which he formed over many years and exhibited frequently.

I well remember the opening sale in our new salesrooms at Progressive Building, Sitwell Street, Derby - a valuable one as befitted the occasion. It was 20th January, 1979 and Derbyshire was snowbound. It had been blowing a blizzard all night and we awaited the arrival of the buyers with some trepidation. Gradually they filtered in from Manchester, Leeds, Birmingham and London – by their surprised expressions they had all expected to make a killing in a nearly empty room. In the event we had a cracking sale!

Many and varied were the collections we sold during the 1970s. I recall J.A. (Alfie) Grant of Edinburgh, a stalwart of the Canadian Philatelic Society of Great Britain. Apart from his formidable Canadian material he had also formed a fine British colonial collection. I remember that in the same sale an accumulation of nearly fifty 'Boxer Rebellion' covers, which had never been on the market before, excited great interest.

Then there were the "HART" collections which we sold and which were to prove one of the most valuable properties that we have handled. W.R. (Bill) Hart was of course well known not only in this country but also in South Africa, which he visited frequently. As a Postal Historian of repute he was both a collector and dealer. The book "The Postal Markings of Natal" in which he collaborated with B.A. Kantey and Leslie Leon is a monumental work.

I had known Bill for many years, both as an auction customer and as a fellow member of the Society of Postal Historians. We were good friends although not perhaps close friends. It was therefore somewhat of a surprise when his solicitor 'phoned me a few days after his sudden death. This was to say that he had directed that I, personally, should handle the sale of his philatelic properties. Bill was noted for his collection and stocks of Boer War and Natal material, but I was amazed by the wealth of other Commonwealth stamps and covers which I found when I made a preliminary valuation. This took some eight or nine days during four visits to his home in Shrewsbury as, at the time, I was getting fit again after a stroke and was obliged to perform a little more slowly than usual. The stamps and postal history material was stored all over the house in steel cupboards, filing cabinets, drawers, under beds and in the roof. It was a fascinating exercise. The material was sold in one major sale, and as part of several later sales over a period of a few months. Bill's widow, Sheila, continued with her own business dealing in postcards, all with a postal history flavour, at stamp fairs in many parts of the country, until sadly she died a few years later.

W.R. (Bill) Hart

The stamp market has always been, to an extent, cyclical. During the years leading up to the 1980 International Exhibition held in London, it gradually achieved boom proportions. This situation could not last and the early 1980s saw a slump in prices of massive proportions. This did not, however, affect items of postal history, which continued progressing upwards - after all, nearly every item of postal history is, in itself, unique. It was at this time, in sale number 351, that we offered the Kenneth Perrin collection of Hong Kong and Treaty Ports.

It had been some years since a major collection of the area had been sold by auction and so we expected some unusual results. We were not to be disappointed. About 75% of the sale went to buyers in Hong Kong, Singapore and Malaya at prices far exceeding our published estimates. One item, Hong Kong S.G. 55c of 1898, comes to mind. At that time the stamp was catalogued about £50 – this was on cover and we placed an estimate of £150. A Mr. Lee 'phoned from Hong Kong with a bid of five thousand pounds on the lot – but confidently hoped it would make less! On sale day two agents were bidding in the room and the item realized £5,400. On the following Monday Mr.Lee 'phoned for his results. He was understandably shocked that his high bid had been unsuccessful. *"Did Richard Chan get it?"* he asked. We explained that we did not disclose the names of successful buyers without permission, but we could tell him that Richard Chan did not get it – to which he replied *"well that's all right then"!*

Sadly Kenneth died in a motor accident shortly before the sale. He was a man of considerable charm who mixed a ferocious gin and dry martini. He had acute intelligence, his other hobbies being bridge and deciphering mediaeval shorthand at the British Museum. He would also sometimes attend at the G.C.H.Q. in Cheltenham to assist in breaking new codes.

Our Third Appearance at a London International Exhibition

The latter part of May 2000 proved to be a philatelic feast commencing with the Canadian P.S. of Great Britain Convention at Hove, lasting for four days. Because the International STAMPSHOW 2000 at Earls Court followed immediately afterwards there were more Canadian members over than usual. This resulted in some splendid liquid reunions.

The President, Colin Banfield, had arranged a fine and varied programme with visits to Arundel Castle and Brighton Pavilion. Apart from sundry mini-displays from members, the major displays included a slide show by Joe Smith of Alberta *"My great uncle's participation in the Canadian Siberian Expeditionary Force"; "Underneath the Arches"* by David Sessions (more technical than it sounds); *"Trans-Atlantic Mail"* offered jointly by Dorothy Sanderson and Malcolm Montgomery and, of course, the very fine *"President's Display"*. Special events for the ladies included a theatre visit and a talk *"My year as the Mayor of Brighton"* by Mrs Jenny Langston.

The final day, Saturday, 20th May, was slightly more formal with the A.G.M., judges' reports on the competitive displays and the annual auction. Finally the banquet – the usual convivial affair, the guest of honour being that doyen of Spanish philately, Ronald Shelley. I had the honour and great pleasure to propose the Toast to the Ladies – they grow in splendour year by year.

My wife Pam and I played truant one day to lunch at Wheeler's fish restaurant in Brighton. Perusing the menu Pam remarked what a pity it was not her birthday or she would have chosen the Lobster Thermidor. Of course we had to back-date the birthday; the lobster, together with a bottle of Chablis, made it a memorable day in more ways than one.

These Canadian affairs are always so enjoyable especially meeting old friends. This year I was so glad to see Stan Lum, the last time being in Toronto three years ago. He was in his usual good form. I still have in my study the jade dolphin which he gave me the year I was President of the Society. Stan writes prolifically on various aspects of Canadian philately and postal history under the pseudonym "The Yellow Peril"!

Stan Lum

And so on to London and Earls Court. The Exhibits were uniformly of the usual brilliant standard and I found time was at a premium to do justice to them all. It was a particular pleasure to see so many friends achieving high awards. The dealers' stands appeared to be doing excellent business and I managed to buy one or two items. Sadly the Millennium Club was a disappointment not only to me but also to those who had worked so hard to organise and market it. It was too big an area for the comparatively small number of members who used it. There was no bar although house wine could be purchased at the food counter, where the choice of food was very small. However this is a small criticism of an otherwise splendid exhibition.

As always my greatest pleasure was in meeting old friends who were visiting the Cavendish Stand, and elsewhere in the hall. Almost on arrival I ran into Edward and Judy Jarvis whom I had met in San Francisco two years earlier.

Ken Chapman

A very welcome early arrival at our Stand was Ken Chapman, so very well known to older collectors and dealers. Ken and his late wife "Dot" were among my earliest and closest friends in the stamp world soon after the war. Before the war Selfridges had a large stamp department and several dealers who later became prominent in the stamp trade started there. Ken was one of these. He soon realized that philatelic journalism was his forte and it was not long before he became editor of *"Stamp Collecting"*, the foremost philatelic magazine of its day. His writings have not been confined to that magazine and it is fair to say that he became the best known philatelic writer not only in Britain but also overseas. In his capacity as editor he and his wife attended international exhibitions in many countries, and he also played an important part in the organization of the 1960 and 1970 Exhibitions here. I was at his 90th birthday lunch a couple of years ago.

I find travel exhilarating, but often thirsty work. (Sri Lanka, 2001)

CHAPTER 3

Overseas Connections and Travel

As the reputation of Cavendish became known abroad, we made a number of business visits to overseas clients, as well as some trips that were pure holiday.

I think our first overseas client was a Dr Immerzeer in Sumatra. He approved of the British and collected the British Empire practically to the exclusion of anything else. For many years he successfully bought in every sale and, presumably, was buying elsewhere as well. Eventually he moved back to Holland and continued to bid from there. At no time can I remember any correspondence passing between us. We would simply receive a bid form and subsequently the cheque when he had made a successful purchase - which happened frequently. It was therefore a surprise when he 'phoned us one morning towards the end of 1973. He was now a Judge in Enschede and would be retiring shortly. He desired us to go over and collect the stamps which would be a substantial lot in several suitcases. It was arranged that I would take the brake over the following week. My wife, who had not been to Holland before, announced her intention to come as well, no doubt to keep an eye on me! We duly crossed to the Hook of Holland, then onward to a country hotel near Enschede, taking in a visit to the Bridge at Arnhem en route. Later we visited Dr Immerzeer and his attractive young wife at their home. The following day, a Sunday, we repaired to his chambers in Enschede where the stamps were kept in an enormous safe. Unfortunately the safe refused to open and, as in England, locksmiths were difficult to find on Sundays. We filled in a few moments of waiting time by eating a minute picnic which his wife had provided. I'm sure it was very health-giving. Meanwhile my wife was enjoying an interesting day out with Mrs Immerzeer.

Eventually we departed with the stamps and we all had dinner at my hotel. Dr Immerzeer enquired if we were returning direct to England the next day. I said we planned to spend a few days in Amsterdam first, to which he replied *"not with my stamps - Amsterdam is full of thieves and vagabonds"*, or words to that effect - well he ought to know. Eventually it was agreed that we would go North and return via the Zuider Zee spending two nights at, I think, Hoorn en route. The collections were off-loaded and kept under lock and key in our bedroom and I 'phoned Dr. Immerzeer to advise all was safe. Back in England the dreaded V.A.T. had arrived and H.M. Customs at Harwich (or was it Felixstowe) did not appear to know how to treat a large consignment of stamps which had not been purchased but were destined for sale by auction, and it was about two hours before the matter was resolved.

The whole exercise had proved well worthwhile. It was interesting and instructive. The collections were sold over some three sales at good prices and we settled with the vendor who was then in Australia.

The Philatelic Congress of Great Britain had been an annual event for most of the twentieth century apart from interruptions during both World Wars. I suppose I must have attended thirty to forty over the years. The earlier Congresses tended to be more social than those of recent years and many are particularly memorable to me.

The highlight of the Folkestone Congress in 1970 was our trip to Boulogne to meet many of our French colleagues. It was the intention that we should cross by hydrofoil, but fog in the Channel obliged us to travel by slow ferry and the bars on board were well patronised. Many of the ladies were elegantly hatted and spurred - Eve Townsend, wife of Bill (previously President of the Royal), was particularly so. It was not long before her chapeau was confiscated by the late (Bojo) Bojanowicz R.D.P. of Poland fame. He continued to wear it until our return to England that night. It was his legendary charm that enabled him to get away with almost anything with the ladies.

On arrival at Boulogne a reception had been laid on at the Maíré. This was the signal for the very many long and boring after-dinner speeches which are obligatory on such occasions. The Press and photographers were much in evidence. Cyril Harmer and I spotted a long table at the back of the room laden with glasses and champagne on ice. We repaired to this and were made very welcome while the speeches droned on and on. With many a "Vive la France" our glasses were refilled. The rest of the visit to France, including the superb lunch, passed in a pleasant haze.

Some days later, after our return home, someone sent me a copy of the Boulogne evening paper. Oddly enough there was no report of the actual visit, or of the innumerable speeches, but there was a large picture on the front page. It showed Cyril and me with glasses held high and the simple caption, "Les philatelistes anglais!"

The following year the Congress itself was held in France, at Enghien, north of Paris. This was to prove a splendidly convivial affair. The Mayor of Enghien had declared it British Week. Union Jacks were much in evidence and most shops were decorated with bunting. We had brought with us a real live London 'bobby' and a Scot's piper. They were both popular in and around the town. John Whiteside and Bernard Lucas did much to foster the Anglo-French entente-cordiale. Their small hotel was the scene of parties that went on for the most of each night, attended not only by delegates but by many of the locals who happened to be passing by! The week ended with a fine banquet followed by a fireworks display.

The Chaiman of Congress (me!) with Distinguished Philatelists, Eastbourne, 1987.

At the end of 1970 my late wife and I spent a happy month in South Africa. It was a memorable trip in many ways. Although principally a holiday I was able to take the opportunity to meet several of our customers in that country. We spent the first few days in Johannesburg before going on to Cape Town.

Cavendish as a company, during fifty years of life and millions of pounds of sales, has been fortunate in being almost free of bad debts. We did, however, have two such debtors in South Africa and I resolved to chase them up. The first was in Johannesburg itself. The individual concerned was a dealer in gold and his premises were awash with gold jewellery, gold coins etc. Despite this he maintained that he was unable to settle our quite modest account. He also refused to return the lots in question *as it would spoil my collection"!!!* This excuse really ruined my lunch. In the end we were obliged to sue in order to obtain payment.

The other case is worth describing as, in a way, it was pure theatre. The customer in this case was a West German with whom we had perfectly satisfactory dealings for several years. He then moved to South Africa and after a few transactions he failed to answer letters or communicate in any way. He had taken up residence in Pretoria and I drove there in a hired car. He was installed in a modern flat in an attractive complex on the outskirts of the city. I noted that his car parking space was unoccupied but the concierge advised me that he would probably return in about an hour. I duly returned at about 5.45 p.m. and went up to his flat. He was surprised when I announced myself and was disinclined to admit me. Eventually, after some argument in which I pointed out that I had come several thousand miles to see him, he reluctantly asked me in to a large and beautifully furnished room. He explained that it was not convenient to see me that day, nor even to discuss the purpose of my visit – and in any case he had no money! We seemed to have reached an impasse when suddenly from behind a large piece of furniture or screen a naked coloured girl appeared and ran across the room before disappearing through another door. For a few moments nothing was said while we both took stock of this situation. He then said *"I no longer collect stamps, I have other interests"* – a rather unnecessary observation in the circumstances. *"I think I will ask you to sell my stamps"*.

We parted quite amicably and I took with me some seven or eight volumes of stamps for which he declined to accept a receipt, being so anxious to accelerate my departure. My wife, who was in the car said *"That was quick – what happened?"* I said *"You won't believe me when I tell you!"* The stamps were sold and in due course, after deductions for charges and car hire, the proceeds were remitted to Pretoria. Debt collecting must be a most disagreeable occupation but I can look back on that day as a not unpleasant and, indeed, noteworthy exercise.

We spent a large part of the holiday with one of Mary's cousins. Reg was a vintage-car enthusiast, his particular pride and joy being a 1926 Bentley which he would drive in the Cape to Kenya rallies. He was also a great and knowledgeable lover of wild life and he took us on an unforgettable tour of various game-reserves through Zululand, Swaziland, Kruger, Sabie and back to Johannesburg. This was in a venerable Alvis. On one occasion in Zululand we were stopped by an old lady who rushed out of the bush – her purpose to sell us a matchbox containing a dead insect of some kind. To our surprise Reg talked and joked with her in fluent Zulu - when we remarked on this he explained that he had spoken Zulu almost before English. He had a Zulu nanny and used to play with her little boy. Sadly Reg died earlier this year just before I was to take my wife Pamela out to meet him. It was perhaps typical that he was watching the Australian Grand Prix on television when it happened. He was one of the kindest men I had ever met.

At the time of our tour the game-reserve in Swaziland was comparatively under-developed and not visited by large organised parties. The roadways were little more than sandy tracks but the weather was hot and dry. We were supplied with a guard in a tattered old army uniform and armed with a .303 rifle. I asked him if he had ever had occasion to use it but he said *"No"* – they were not supplied with ammunition.

Swaziland proved to be full of surprises. As we proceeded along the unmade road we reached a rough sign marked "Holiday Inn" pointing into the bush; this we followed. It proved to be similar to Holiday Inns the world over, except for some of the clientele. We went down for drinks before dinner to find the three barmen, obviously terrified, huddled at one end of the bar. They were providing free drink to a real-life witch doctor, very smelly and festooned with bones and sundry dead things – we did not stay. At that time casinos were not permitted in South Africa but there was one in Mbabane and South Africans would regularly fly in there to gamble. This was no doubt a considerable help to the Swaziland economy. We went to the casino that evening and our friend the witch-doctor was already there, playing the fruit machines and now very drunk. He was being supplied with cash by a frightened attendant. We learnt that he would come down from the hills and put in an appearance every month or so.

At that time Barclays Bank was the only three-storey building in Mbabane. The Government buildings were opposite and the main street parking lot was marked out with reservations for "His Majesty the King", "The Prime Minister", "The Chancellor of the Exchequer" etc. There was a small covered market and I was tempted by a sign outside which said "This way for stamps". The stall sold mixed packets of used low value Swaziland, South African and Mozambique material. The proprietrix told me she was the biggest stamp dealer in Swaziland. I had no reason to question this as she must have been every bit of 25 stone! I bought a few packets but declined the snake-skin and assorted small dried creatures which she also offered me.

On the return journey a night was spent at the Sabie River. The next day, en route for Johannesburg, we diverted to look at a long-deserted mining township. The tombstones in the cemetery indicated that the population had been mainly of Welsh origin. The inscriptions were generally stark and to the point, *"Drowned when in drink"*, *"Stabbed in a brawl"* and such like. While walking round the seemingly deserted graveyard we were startled by an enormous character who suddenly rose up from behind a tombstone. He had been drinking from a bucket of dark brown liquid and was no doubt the self-appointed custodian of the place. He followed us round intoning repeatedly *"Everybody dead, all your fathers, all your mothers, everybody dead"*. We finally bought him off with a couple of packets of cigarettes.

Three days later we were in England – and before long, I was back on the rostrum.

The high spot of 1999 for my wife and myself was an extended holiday in the U.S.A. This commenced with two weeks in Arizona which were a delight and passed all too quickly. My cousin Pat went to the States as a G.I. bride, she then proceeded to found a dynasty. Her three daughters have all produced families and so I had the pleasure of meeting sundry second cousins and cousins once removed. One even collected stamps! Their lovely homes high in the woods above Prescott were away from the sometimes arid heat of the plains and desert. A full programme had been organized for us and there was much to see. The intellectual side was not forgotten including a geological walk (optional!) conducted by, I think, someone from Phoenix University.

An hour's flight in a light plane over the Grand Canyon was an exciting experience and is to be recommended. Our stay ended with a family dinner party at a Prescott hotel which dates back to Frontier days. The bullet holes from the last shoot-out are still visible. I suspect that every time the place is redecorated, a few shots are put in the ceiling – or is this an unworthy thought? From Prescott we headed for San Francisco, taking in the Hoover Dam and the obligatory two nights in Las Vegas – the latter a city of fantasy which did not belie its reputation.

The Tuscan Inn at Fisherman's Wharf proved to be a splendid choice of hotel. The restaurant was so good that we used it several times in spite of the excellent choice of fish restaurants in the Wharf area. Our stay in San Francisco was made for us by our friends Gavin and Janice Lobman. I met Gavin and Janice three years ago at the International Exhibition in Toronto. Gavin collects Canada but his particular interest is currently Irish postal history. He is a national judge and I envied his extensive philatelic library. The Lobmans transported us to many of the galleries and places of interest in and around the city. A memorable day was spent at the Pebble Beach Golf Club – home of the Bob Hope Classic – where we dined in the opulent Club House.

Early in 1979 I went over to the Isle of Man to take delivery of the A.L.A. Bonbernard 'Mauritius'. Mr. Bonbernard had spent much of his life in the former colony and was enjoying his retirement in a home of real character with wonderful gardens. What was also interesting to me was that I stayed in the same hotel where I had been quartered in 1942 on a course. Possibly unique in Army catering was the fact that the management remained in situ to look after and feed us. It was an idyllic three months. Another visit to I.O.M. was made to collect Tony Raybon's extensive British Commonwealth collection. He had been a buyer at our sales for many years and took up residence in Douglas when he retired from farming.

My most recent trip abroad was in 2001, a week after my eightieth birthday, when we went to Sri Lanka, or Ceylon as I still prefer to call it - perhaps because I once collected the pence issues or perhaps simply it's the old reactionary coming out in me. As a stamp collector many of the sights were already familiar - Lion Rock, the Temple of the Tooth, Adam's Peak, tea plantations and of course elephants galore. Twelve of our party undertook what was proclaimed to be "a daring and adventurous ride through virgin jungle on Sri Lanka elephants". We were distributed upon three elephants and it proved to be a hilarious experience. We followed a path through the "Virgin Jungle" and after about a quarter of a mile our elephant halted and a small boy ran out of the bush flourishing a bunch of bananas. These we had to buy to feed the elephant or else it would not agree to continue the journey. This routine was repeated at intervals. It was small wonder that all the elephants suffered from flatulence and broke wind noisily, often in unison.

My wife Pam aloft in 2001.

I would happily return to Sri Lanka. The beauty of the island is captivating and the people invariably smiling and friendly. We arrived just as the first test match was in progress at Colombo. We lost by an innings and many runs. Everyone there enjoys talking cricket and I was discussing the match with one of the staff at our hotel. On my remarking that they were too good for us he replied *"Oh, no England were very unlucky"*. Surely the understatement of the year. *"And the umpiring was very bad; Indians you know"!!*

Education is taken very seriously by the Sri Lankan Government and equally so by parents. I had the opportunity to visit the school in one of the small towns we passed through. It comprised departments for both small children and the seniors taking both 'O' and 'A' Levels for boys and for girls. Schooling is free for all and everything including school uniforms is supplied by the Government. While I was there an inter-school cricket match was in progress all properly attired. The whole set-up was reminiscent of a good English pre-war grammar school. Because of these high educational standards, I was told that Sri Lanka suffers a brain drain. The medical profession in particular is able to command much higher salaries overseas. While we were there my wife unfortunately had an accident and was well cared for by local G.Ps. An X-Ray was necessary which cost all of £7.50! A similar one taken on our return home cost £98.

CHAPTER 4

Friends, Clients and Eccentrics

London Dealers

As I have remarked before, during the pre-World War II years and for several years afterwards, it was not customary for philatelic auctioneers to publish valuations in their auction catalogues. Because of this there was very little postal bidding, and therefore it could result in a free-for-all in the room - I do not mean physical!

During the immediate post-war years there were stamp auctions almost every day of the week in London – sometimes two or more on the same day. Some interesting, lively and indeed odd characters frequented the salerooms. At that time I was actually in London for two days every other week and it was my good fortune to experience the saleroom atmosphere which then existed.

My frequent forays there during the late forties and fifties were always enjoyable and often exciting. There were many 'characters' among the regular auction-goers and I made several friends. As a mere 'provincial' I found the London scene infinitely more interesting than I do today. I remember the Festival year of 1952 with its hot summer, the Festival Gardens and, of course, Emmet's Guiness Clock. The expenditure in taxpayers' money was infinitesimal compared with that spent on the now infamous Millennium Dome - a project of dubious worth if ever there was one. The several auction houses ensured that there were sales or viewing most days of the week and the journey from Derbyshire was never wasted.

How well I remember Harmers with the late Cyril wending his amiable, laconic way through a three-day sale which could easily have been completed in one!! Then there was Harmer Rookes, subsequently taken over by Gibbons. The auctioneer was adept at spotting bids on the chandelier. I remember one occasion where only two of us were left in the room towards the end of a sale. We were quietly chatting together, but the bidding still droned on - five pounds, ten, fifteen, twenty pounds! Needless to say, this devious kind of thing rarely happens in today's auction rooms, because it is easy to detect by experienced auction-goers.

Robson Lowe was then in Pall Mall, renowned for the quality of his sales and the efficiency of his lady auctioneers. Pall Mall sales also afforded me the opportunity to visit Berry Bros. & Rudd round the corner in St. James's Street to replenish my stock of their "Good Ordinary Claret" which they continue to send me to this day.

I always enjoyed Plumridge's sales. Frank Hadlow ran them with the assistance of his sister and a Mr. Mounser - I expect all now have passed on. Frank, and his father before him, had very many philatelist friends of the old school, and because of this he was entrusted with the sale of many fine collections which might have otherwise gone elsewhere. The premises were in Archer Street, the Windmill Theatre being at the corner. The large saleroom and the office occupied all of the first floor, while above and below were rehearsal rooms. Sales were obliged to compete with tap dancing, bands of various kinds and singers but, like the Windmill itself, sales went on.

On sale days the viewing ceased at one o'clock and Frank Hadlow, accompanied by some five or six members of the philatelic drinking classes, would adjourn to a hostelry in nearby Rupert Street. At ten minutes to two Frank would arise from his place at the corner of the bar and announce that he would sell Lot One at precisely two o'clock. Many were the friendships I made at Plumridges during those early days and especially I remember Thomas Watts. Occasionally early covers would turn up addressed to Winch Bros. The three brothers, John Miller, George Henry and Frederick William Winch, were at school in the 1860s. All three were avid stamp collectors and accumulated many duplicates which they decided to advertise for sale. The response led to the establishment of the House of Winch in 1870. In 1880 the Paris branch of Winch Frères was opened at No. 6, Rue Royale and this was shortly followed by branches in Cannes, Menton and Nice. In 1884 the London branch opened at 24, Old Bond Street. The two younger brothers died in 1898 and 1904, but John continued the business. On his retirement in 1926 he disposed of his interests to Tommy Watts who continued the operation from Dovercourt.

Tommy attended all London sales and, if he had to attend viewing elsewhere, his charming wife would bid for him. His main interest was classical and early material from many countries. He would buy old collections, mixed lots and single-country lots which he would re-mount, write up and place in other sales. On one occasion he bought a shoe-box containing a quantity of Greece Hermes heads on pieces. These he rearranged and wrote up into some twenty lots. When sold by the same auction house they fetched some five or six times the original cost. When I started Cavendish Auctions a few years later, Tommy became our first regular vendor and upon his death we sold a significant proportion of his stock.

'Tiny' Moore was a large and familiar figure at these early post-war sales in London. He was what I would term a 'Dealers' dealer' and was always accompanied by two large suitcases into which he would regularly add and subtract stock. When not at a sale, he would spend the day calling on West End and City dealers. We sometimes had a bar-lunch together and I remember his particular liking for potato salad with everything.

From *"Stamp Collecting"* 1926

The name of Houtzamer may be familiar as it appears on many Expert Certificates of the period. He had an encyclopaedic knowledge of classic European material. He was also a pleasant and kindly man and was generous in imparting his expertise to others. I sometimes had the good fortune to sit next to him at sales. His specialised stock was sold by several salerooms after his death - I have always felt with precipitate haste. The extensive Whitfield King stock suffered a similar fate. There is a good case to be made for collectors to sell all or part of their collections during their lifetimes when they are still able to exercise control over the disposal.

Colonel "Wattie", so called because his every sentence ended in "what, what", sounding somewhat like a stage colonel, was a dear man of considerable charm. He was always to be seen in the salerooms. He came up to London every weekday and divided his time between auctions and the Royal. We met frequently and struck common ground in that I live in Matlock and during the war he was there commanding the Intelligence Corps O.C.T.U. at Smedley's Hydro.

Dr. Bauer of the Westminster Stamp Co. specialised in U.S.A. and was a thorn in the flesh to any collector of that country attending the sale. He purchased literally any U.S. material of merit which appeared on the market for many years. His favourite ploy was to lurk outside the saleroom door until the first U.S. lot came up. He would then suddenly appear and start bidding, thereby creating a psychological advantage over the rest of the room. Most of his purchases were exported to the U.S. and this probably accounts for the paucity of such material over here to this day.

This narrative would not be complete without the mention of "Johnny" Johnson of Fleet Street, without doubt the leading dealer and authority on line-engraved G.B. for some decades. Originally in partnership with a Mr. Readhead, the agreement when they parted was that Readhead took the 'blues' and Johnson kept the 'blacks'. That is not to say that Johnson was exclusively G.B.; he also had a vast British Empire stock including much proof material. He was a very complex character. If he liked you he was the kindest of men. If he did not, he was best avoided. I first met him at Harmer Rookes and he invited me round to his offices after the sale. There I met the late Dr. Wiggins for the first time and the three of us crossed the road for tea at the Lyons opposite.

This ritual was repeated on many occasions. Johnny's son 'young Johnny', or Dan as he was known, was the chief of Combustion Research at Rolls-Royce in Derby. We became close friends but it was the father whom I had met first. I had many a session looking through his stockbooks and he taught me a lot. Afterwards our next port of call was usually the Cock Tavern, often followed by a taxi somewhere for dinner.

It was Johnny's proud boast that he was known by every taxi driver in London - I think he was probably right. One evening when we were about to leave for the Cock Tavern, a well known and rather pompous collector entered the office and Johnny said he could join us if he so wished. On his desk was a pile of some thirty or forty sheets of small star watermarked paper. The newcomer's eyes alighted upon these and Johnny said that as a special favour he could have a sheet for £5. The deal done, he then departed to wash his hands before we went out. Returning with dripping hands, he looked round then picked up several of the watermarked sheets to dry them - such was his puckish sense of humour. I have said that the stamp world had many 'characters' and for me, Johnny was certainly the greatest.

It is inevitable that as I write these notes I should recall persons and happenings that may have taken place 50 or 60 years ago. There was, for example, Mr Charlton from Manchester who would visit us in Derby even before the advent of Cavendish Auctions. He was a philatelist of the old school who collected line-engraved Great Britain and other classics. It was his proud boast that he could spot a re-entry in a stamp shop window from the other side of the street!

Bruce Auckland was an incredible fellow. He had an immense knowledge of Scottish postal history and was also a Fellow of the Canadian Philatelic Society of G.B. At one time he was a regular attender at Congress where we first met. One year when Congress was being held at Norwich we spent an enjoyable day together on the Broads. He died at the age of 102 and his interest in matters philatelic and postal history had endured to the end. During his last few years we had sold some significant parts of his collection.

The 1960s & 1970s

The late Harold Bruce Macmillan joined the printing firm of R B Macmillan Ltd., founded by his father after the First World War, in 1923. When his father died in 1933 Harold became Chairman and Managing Director. In his young days he was a noted motor-cyclist competing in National and International events. In 1929 he was a member of the James Motor Cycle Company Team in the International 6-Day Trial on the Continent. Under Harold's leadership his firm made considerable progress and commenced specialising in multi-colour printing and producing labels. I remember visiting the factory on one occasion and watching a huge machine producing Guinness labels. These came out like enormous sheets of stamps which then passed to a guillotine machine. The machine worked 24 hours a day making its contribution to the thirst of Guinness lovers.

During W.W.II Harold was commissioned into the Royal Engineers and engaged mainly in the specialised production of maps, for which activity he was commended by the GOC Middle East, General Paget, when he concluded his Army service in 1946.

After the War Harold made several trips to the West Indies which resulted in nearly all the labels required for Rum bottles produced in the islands being supplied by Macmillans. He made splendid collections of all the West Indian colonies, especially of early issues to Geo. V. His collections covered the entire Empire but apart from B.W.I. his special interests were in the West African colonies. When we sold his collection following his death it proved to be the greatest single contribution to the not inconsiderable estate. He had brought to his philatelic interests the same expertise which he applied to his business and charitable interests. At the time of his death he was a trustee of the Macmillan Cancer Relief Fund which had been founded by an uncle. Yet another interest was gardening and as well as flowers he produced vast quantities of fruit and vegetables, most of which were given away.

Harold Macmillan

I met Harold very soon after I started my own business in Derby in 1947. He and his wife Beth became close and valued friends with Mary and myself, and I had the honour to become his Executor and Trustee.

In a regimental magazine recently the editor was inviting articles of interesting, exciting, unusual or humorous vein about experiences during W.W.II I thought at once of the late Peter Moore. His experience could fulfil all of these categories. Peter was a baker in Matlock and I met him very soon after we came here in 1947. He always at that time had a slight and pleasant aroma of freshly baked bread. He was a collector and formed very good collections of such diverse subjects as Great Britain and Rhodesia, both of which we sold in due time. Peter's unforgettable experience came about the middle of the War. He was the rear-gunner, "tail-end Charlie", of a bomber returning from a raid over Germany. They were shot down over Holland and he managed to bail out. This was at night and he made an awkward landing in a field, breaking a leg in the process. Soon after dawn he became aware that a main road ran adjacent to the field in which he lay. He was also acutely aware that he needed medical attention. He managed to crawl to the side of the road where a great deal of military traffic was passing up and down, including lorries packed with German troops and smaller vehicles. Realising that he had no option but to give himself up he kept waving to the passing trucks. Although one or two Germans waved back, they otherwise showed no interest in this enemy airman. Eventually a farmer came along in his horse and cart and picked him up. He was taken back to the farm and given food before being handed over to the Dutch police who took him to hospital.

The rest of the War was spent in a P.O.W. camp. Peter was a lovely man and his untimely death came some 15 years ago while working on his allotment. He had had a heart attack and it was some time before he was found.

It was at the Queen's Hotel in Manchester that we encountered the "Rolling Stones". In those early days we would arrive at our venue, together with the sale material, at about 10.30 a.m. On this occasion we found the hotel entrance besieged by some hundreds of teenagers, mainly screaming girls. George, the Head Porter, and his staff were valiantly defending his domain. *"It's them Rolling Stones"* he said. *"Good job you were not here last night!"* We eventually got inside and got the "view" underway prior to the sale, scheduled to commence at 2 p.m. We would arrange for the staff to have lunch in two sittings, my wife and the girls going first. When they returned, my wife said *"It's pandemonium down there - you'd better watch your bill!"* When the rest of us went down, it was clear that the "Stones" had contrived to create chaos in the dining room. My wife's warning proved to be prophetic because a few days later I received the Rolling Stones' account for their stay, and presumably they had been sent the modest bill incurred by Cavendish.

During 1969/70 I was President of the Derby Philatelic Society and I invited a prominent young philatelist to come and show his splendid Great Britain collection which had been awarded the Silver Mail Coach at Stampex that year. He stayed with us on our Derbyshire hillside and in the morning he appeared in running gear, proposing a little exercise before breakfast. It was a day in November when hill fogs are prevalent. We bade him farewell as he departed in fine style into the mist. Breakfast time came and went and we were about to report a missing person when he appeared in late morning. He had been lost and remote farms where he called had been unable to help. He would not forget his visit to Derbyshire!

I have enjoyed my life in my chosen career, and most of all the friends I have made. I first met the late 'Steph' Stobbs during the 1970s and was privileged to become one of his vast circle of friends in the Midlands. He was a little man with a big heart and a squeaky voice. As well as being a connoisseur of whisky, he was a postal historian par excellence and a Past President of the Society of Postal Historians. About twice a year I used to meet 'Steph' in company with the late Ted Coles and other members of the Birmingham postal history fraternity for a very convivial lunch at the "Gipsy Tent" on the road to Kidderminster. 'Steph' had many interests, the greatest of which was Military Mail with Boer War and P.O.W. Mail in particular. He also formed collections of various aspects of Midlands postal history, of Australia and also of Masonic material, all of which created tremendous interest when we sold them from time to time.

'Steph' Stobbs

'Bob' Warren

Another friend, 'Bob' Warren, will be remembered with affection by many of our auction buyers. He attended nearly every sale from about 1960 until his death some three years ago. He had formed a vast general Commonwealth collection which we eventually sold. We usually had lunch together on viewing days. His boisterous good humour masked some years of chronic ill health and his arrival at our reception was always heralded by uproar. He had been a gallant soldier and I once asked about his award of the Military Cross in Northern Europe. This produced great mirth and typically he attributed it all to his Sergeant who won a Military Medal in the same action. He was indeed a very special and lovely man.

Our sales in Manchester and Leeds brought us many friends from Red and White Rose Country and whilst writing I find that memories of so many characters come to mind. During 1975/76 we sold the Vine stock. Kenneth Vine was a man of great charm. He took early retirement with the intention of dealing in stamps, which he loved, and spent some three years building up a stock of quality material, then sadly he died before his new business could get underway. He was a connoisseur and his artistry extended to his garden which was adorned with several small stone figures - one of which now has a favoured place in my own garden.

Cyril Baker was another Yorkshireman who will be remembered. Always immaculately dressed he seldom missed one of our Leeds sales. Yorkshire Postal History and especially Halifax was his deep interest, which we had the privilege of selling after his death. I was reminded of this when some items from his collection turned up again in a sale a year or two ago.

Yet another Yorkshire pair who I remember with affection were Messrs. Heseldine, who collected West Indies, and Ormerod who aided and abetted. They attended all our sales in Yorkshire almost from the beginning. Although they had been friends since school days they always addressed each other as "Mr." - "is that not so Mr. Ormerod? - It is Mr. Heseldine". It was rather like an old-fashioned Music Hall turn! Mr. Heseldine had spent most of his working life with a Bradford firm of solicitors who obviously thought a great deal of him. They were also his executors and told me that he was permitted the run of the cellars and could have anything of a philatelic nature which might be of interest to him. They were more than mildly surprised to learn the value of a penny black collection he had formed as a result of his endeavours!

During 1977/78 there was quite a boom in Australian Commonwealth material and 'Kangaroo' high values soon attracted the attention of the investment fraternity. A major collection which we sold at this time was the property of a retired Yorkshire wool merchant. It was housed in some forty or fifty volumes, all mint, and in immaculate condition. I drove up to Yorkshire to collect the material and could not fail to notice the somewhat alcoholic aroma from the many demi-johns which were bubbling away in the hall. Replying to my enquiry whether making home-made wine was another of his hobbies he said *"Nay lad, it's wife - she's promised to make me a couple of bottles a day as long as I keep off the hard stuff!"*. We went into the vendor's study where the albums were in dust covers on shelving around the wall. Presently his wife arrived with a bottle and glasses on a tray. As she poured out the wine this conversation took place

"And what are we favoured with today my dear?"
"It's parsnip wine".
"Oh, you're in for a treat my lad, it's your lucky day, wife's famous for her parsnip wine".

His wife then said she was going shopping and would return to give us lunch. Meanwhile her husband said not to touch the wine yet - *"let it breathe"*. We inspected one of the albums, then he said *"There she goes!"* - his wife was driving out through the gate. He arose and produced a bottle of vodka from one of the dust covers and laced our drinks accordingly, saying, *"It's the only way I can drink the bloody stuff!"*.

In 1975 we sold the "Miller Collection". The brothers Miller were extremely wealthy and lived together on the outskirts of Manchester. Both home and garden were large and indeed needed to be, because both brothers collected jointly on a grand scale. Although the stamp collection was formidable it was really insignificant compared with the antique furniture, silver, clocks, porcelain, coins, dolls houses etc. which were crammed in duplicated array in the various rooms. In the garden there was even a pagoda-like building which housed the Chinese and Japanese collections. Both brothers had died in their eighties within a few months of each other. My visit to take delivery of the stamps was quite fascinating.

Subsequently, we were asked to arrange the sale of the various portable collections comprising small Far Eastern items, also snuffboxes, coin boxes and a tremendous amount of mechanical toys and other toys including soldiers and Dinky Toys, all in the original boxes as sold. This was the only time we had conducted a sale other than that of stamps and postal history. It was, for me, the most interesting sale I had ever held and attracted a different kind of buyer from all over the country. Every lot sold - for cash and with no necessity for posting away!

There was an amusing sequel to the whole operation. The brothers also collected rare wines which had been left to one of the solicitors handling the Estate. An old gardener had been retained to keep the grounds in good order pending the sale of the property. The cellar where the wines were stored also had access from the garden at the rear of the house. When the beneficiary came to collect his wines he also found a considerable number of empty bottles. It appears that the gardener, showing great discrimination, had been in the habit of enjoying a bottle of Chateau de Rothschild Lafite with his lunch-time sandwiches!

The late Dr Hetherington was a prolific and knowledgeable collector of stamps, covers and philatelic literature. His collections were formidable and, as a bachelor, they occupied most of his waking time. He also had an appetite for curry - the hottest possible - which I once shared with almost fatal results! His collections were kept at his flat and also at a local depository. When we collected the material for sale in 1972 it required two journeys to Worthing, one with a hired van. Dr Hetherington was not a medical doctor and we had often wondered the nature of his doctorate and this was now revealed. His diploma as Dr. of Philately had been awarded by an obscure university in Texas.

In the early seventies, about the time when we opened a new sale room in the Wardwick, Derby, we sold a splendid mint West Indies collection on behalf of a retired clergyman in Somerset. A few years later this gentleman telephoned me. He was sending me his collection of penny blacks and two penny blues for early sale by auction, and requested an advance of £1,000 by return which he needed to put on a horse. The Grand National was due to take place in a few days time. Not only was this a rather odd request but he also sounded strange and excited on the 'phone. In the event I felt it wise to delay sending the advance. This was just as well because the horse, a 40 to 1 chance, fell at one of the early fences. A few days later the collection of blacks and blues arrived. They were superb examples, including multiples, but all the gems had suffered by having been heavily written upon the back with a blue Biro pen. Another example of what might have been! Shortly afterwards I heard from this gentleman's son-in-law. His father-in-law had, in fact, had a breakdown and would we sell the rest of his collection? This we did and fortunately it had not been vandalised in any way.

Jack Steward was one of the several memorable characters who were members of the Birmingham Philatelic Society. Some of our earliest sales were held in that City and it was here that we first met. He attended all these sales and at the conclusion of the proceedings many of us would adjourn to the bar. Indeed in the 1950's and 60's Cavendish Sales became akin to a club and a hard core of buyers from all over the Midlands would follow us to the various venues. Jack was also a member of the Society of Postal Historians, which at that time included several keen members from the Birmingham area, including Frank Bottomley and the late 'Ted' Coles. The annual conference of the S.P.H. has always been a particularly convivial affair. On the Saturday afternoon it had become the custom for Jack Steward to fill his car with various members and drive at break-neck speed to sundry neighbouring towns in search of book-shops.

The first time the meeting was held at Leamington Spa we followed this now accepted practice, returning in time to change for dinner. Later in the bar Jack departed for bed saying *"This is the best day I have ever had at an S.P.H. Conference"*. The following morning I was met by Frank Bottomley with the sad news that Jack had died during the night Frank had, over the years, become unofficial medical officer of the S.P.H. I think that many members would save up their sundry ailments over the year in order to seek his advice during the Conference. Frank would dispense advice with his customary good humour. He has become a special friend and I look forward to the now all too rare occasions when he comes to stay a few days with us. This is often when my wife is away and we eat and drink in the various excellent Derbyshire country pubs. Frank does not shoot but being game for anything (not a pun) he once accompanied me to a Saturday shoot one bleak November day. It turned out to be one of the wettest days on record and the old waterproofs I was able to supply were quite inadequate. He was uncomplaining but must have hated every minute of it. Happier times were when he would meet my friend, the late Desmond Stoker.

The stories about Desmond are legion and could be the subject of an extended chapter on their own. During the Burma Campaign his Field Ambulance was over-run by the Japanese with almost total casualties. Desmond managed to walk back to India over several weeks and his diary of this ordeal is now at the War Museum. He later returned to Burma and there is a photograph of his surgery deep in the jungle. He is seated on a broken deck chair underneath a large sign advertising "THE QUACKERY". He had many interests including regaling his friends with quantities of sherry which he produced in a solera system made from plastic dustbins in his cellar. At his memorial service the friend giving the address paid this tribute - *"Desmond Stoker was the only man I know who could turn Jeyes Fluid into sherry"*. However, I digress.

The Morecambe Bay area enjoys an equitable climate and is popular with retired people. It used to be well endowed with the stamp collecting fraternity - perhaps it still is. Percy Norman lived in Hest Bank. He was a retired bank official and I first met him in Derby when he was staying with a mutual friend - also a collector. Subsequently we did much business together and I made many journeys to that part of England and enjoyed the hospitality of his charming wife and himself. He was a collector of Great Britain and Commonwealth in some depth and after his death we were entrusted with the sale of this fine collection. An interesting side-light on my association with Percy was that at that time his father-in-law was the oldest man in England. He was, I think, 105 and was cared for by two unmarried daughters. He was still active and would meet his friends daily at the local pub. and this is where he died one morning - an end which many of us would envy!

The late Mr Hassopoulis had a large stamp shop in Charing Cross Road, not far from Leicester Square Tube Station. "Hasso", as he was known, was a familiar figure in all the London salerooms and I was therefore somewhat surprised to receive a telephone call from him one day to say that he was proposing to sell a substantial portion of his stock. He would like it to be offered by us in Derby providing we would give him a 50% advance pending sale. I agreed, provided that I considered the material was saleable and that it was to be offered without reserve. He considered this a satisfactory arrangement and the next morning he duly arrived with three or four large suitcases. I selected most of the material which amounted to several thousands of pounds and duly paid him the agreed advance.

His return train was in the late afternoon so I suggested lunch at the Midland Hotel adjacent to the station, and my wife, who was shopping in Derby that day, joined us. It proved to be a most hilarious lunch-time. Hasso was in very high spirits and entertained us with tales of his philatelic adventures in Eastern Europe before coming to England and setting up in business. His cornering of the entire bogus issue of Azerbaijan in the early twenties and involvement with the many covers which established a degree of authenticity to this issue were recounted amid much merriment. Two or three days later Hasso 'phoned again. He said he was now bankrupt and future dealings were to be with the liquidators – oddly he was still in high good humour!!

The 1980s & 1990s

I have been to all the International Exhibitions in London since 1950 and they have been better each time. London 1980 was the first time we took a stand which proved to be a highly successful exercise. Following the show this is what I wrote:

"This was an exhibition which 'had everything' - collections of the highest quality from practically every country in the world, dealers of many nationalities occupying about 250 Trade Stands, buffets, bars and perhaps most entertaining of all, 'Little Licking Station' which provided continuous fun and games for the young collector - indeed on the Saturday and Sunday the area around Little Licking was reminiscent of Hampstead Heath on a Bank Holiday!"

Our stand at our second London International Exhibition, 1990. James G-T, Frank Laycock and Dave Tarry are happily serving clients, watched at the far left by Harry Dagnall.

For ourselves, we had the opportunity of meeting some hundreds of our friends from all parts of the country and from overseas - this was our greatest pleasure, which was repeated at both the London exhibitions in 1990 and 2000.

The late Ernest Hugen, FRPSL, will be remembered by older collectors. For many years he was Hon. Secretary of the Philatelic Congress of Great Britain, with the devoted assistance of Marjorie Humble. He had built up a formidable collection of Europeans, British Colonials and G.B. All were mint and herein lies an unhappy tale of what might have been. Over the years he became more interested in organised philately - and, indeed, in organising philately, so much so that he eventually lost interest in collecting and the stamps were put into store. Upon his death we were instructed to handle the sale of the collection and duly travelled down to Brighton to take delivery.

The albums had been stored partly in a Bank vault and partly under the stairs at his home. Sadly the larger part of the material was badly foxed or stuck-down and the realisation was a mere fraction of what it would otherwise have been. This was the most extreme example of neglect that I have come across.

Most of us at some time have been a victim of mistaken identity. This once happened to me at the Shire Horse Show at Ashbourne in Derbyshire. I was heading for the beertent when a character emerged and addressed me in Derbyshire-speak:

"Art int Federation then?"
"Er – no, I don't think so"
"Are you sure? – we're all int Federation"
"What sort of Federation is this?"
"Well, Master Butchers' Federation, of course – you are a butcher aren't you?"
"No, I'm not a butcher
"Are you sure?"
"Yes, I'm sure I'm not a butcher"
"I could have sworn you were a butcher – what are you then?"
"I'm an auctioneer"
"GOT IT, I'VE BOUGHT HUNDREDS OF PIGS FROM YOU IN MY TIME"
- and he went happily away!

Shire horse shows do take place in other parts of the country and any opportunity to see these magnificent animals put through their paces should not be missed. At Burton-upon-Trent it is the BASS MUSEUM where the history of this world-famous brewery and artefacts are graphically displayed. The stables housing the Bass shire horses are open for inspection, also meals may be had and of course, the opportunity to sample the ambrosial brew.

The Society of Postal Historians usually hold a one-day meeting at the Bass Museum about every other year. This is convened by Richard Farman who is of course well known for his various studies of Midlands Postal History. What is perhaps less well known is that he is a local historian who played an important part in setting up the Bass Museum.

Of course I have some non-philatelic memories as well. Some years ago readers of the 'DAILY TELEGRAPH' will have noted with some amusement the letter of Dr. Charles Goodsen-Wickes and the subsequent correspondence from readers advising the good doctor on the action he should or might have taken. It seems that Dr. Goodsen-Wickes, in search of a palliative for his 'flu symptoms, entered a pub, where the barman refused to serve him with a "whiskey-mac" of his own particular prescription.

This brings to mind a happy incident described to me by my late father. Apart from multiple wounds received on the Somme and elsewhere in France he was rarely in need of medical attention. However, when in his early eighties, and living alone in West Derby, Liverpool, he felt ill, self diagnosed 'flu, and took to his bed after 'phoning for a doctor. The doctor arrived and confirmed the diagnosis as probably correct. To my father's surprise he then produced a bottle of whiskey from his case, poured out a large slug for dad and one for himself, then joined him in bed to drink it! A few years later the doctor died. He was greatly loved in the West Derby area and the church and grounds were packed to overflowing by people paying their last respects.

My father lived to a great age after spending several agreeable years at a place run by the Officers' Association near Newton Abbot and achieved the distinction of oldest inhabitant. At 90 he once told me that he had lived too long and it was time to go. At 98 he had changed his mind and was looking forward to his century – sadly that was not to be.

Auctions in the early days were family affairs - my father (far left) and my son, Mick (seated) alongside me as I take the rostrum. (Manchester, 1962)

But we should return to stamps….. The Scots have produced many serious philatelists, both in their own country and more especially among the vast number of expatriates. Dr Matthew Carstairs was one of the latter. He lived near Amersham and was a popular member of the Canadian Philatelic Society of Great Britain. In his presidential year he held the Annual Convention in Oxford.

A few years later he died (in 1984 I think) and we were instructed to handle the sale of his wonderful collection. The strength of his Canadian collection was well known, but what we did not know was that this strength was duplicated in several other Commonwealth countries. I made two journeys to Amersham and spent several hours in his stamp room.

This was a fascinating experience as very little of the collection had been mounted, and envelope after envelope yielded "find" after "find". A final trip was made to take delivery, on which occasion I was accompanied by Frank Laycock to whom I had recently sold the business. This time a visit to the bank was necessary to collect some more material which was deposited there.

The whole exercise had been exciting and the sale itself was no less stimulating. The room was packed, including buyers who had flown in from Canada.

Normally at that time our sales commenced at 2.00 p.m. and ended at approximately 5.30 p.m. On this occasion nearly every lot was fought over and the sale was finally completed at 8.30 p.m. I had gained the impression from Mrs Carstairs that she thought rather little of Matthew's collecting activities and certainly he had not given her any indication of the value of the accumulation. It was therefore indeed a pleasure for us to be the bearer of extremely good news after the sale.

Here again is another reason for a philatelist to give his potential beneficiary not only an indication of the value of the collection but also to outline instructions for disposal.

Some Eccentrics

All collecting hobbies attract eccentrics and stamps and postal history are no exception. Let it be said at once that these characters are to be found on both sides of the counter! At Cavendish we have, fortunately, had our share - without the occasional eccentric the world would indeed be a dull place, although they do now seem to be in short supply compared with some years ago.

I can recall two Nottingham collectors, one who collected Red stamps only, while the other considered no stamp was worth more than a penny and this was the limit he would pay. The Red stamp man showed me his collection once. I had no idea there were so many red stamps in the catalogue, but oh, how boring. The 1d stamp collector had, in fact, quite a formidable collection. He would often buy more expensive items but expected to be given a quantity of near worthless stamps so that the sum total would come to not more than 1d each. In this way he would salve his conscience.

The late Charles Loach was an ultra perfectionist. He built up a very fine Empire and Commonwealth collection. His particular, not unworthy, fad was his insistence on perfect centring. He carried a piece of black card and upon this any stamp he was offered was subjected to his centring test. Charles held an important post with British Rail where his expertise was equally meticulous. Apart from this, philately was his life and occupied his free time to the exclusion of everything else. I always felt so sorry for his wife. Charles did not extend his scrupulous fastidiousness to his home, which could have been so nice, but the inside was drab and appeared to have been undecorated from the day he moved in many years before. In later years he turned his attention to postal history. I don't know what was his yardstick for perfection in this case, but it was also a very fine collection.

At this stage I make a plea – please, oh, please don't become a "stamp bore". Have other and wider interests than simply stamps and postal history and enjoy an expanding circle of friends. The alternative is to "enjoy" solely the company of other stamp bores.

On one occasion we had a transvestite bidding at one of our Manchester sales which caused some confusion. I had already knocked down a few lots to a lady with waist length blond hair and wearing a fur coat when Mrs. Kimber, who was clerking, whispered in my ear *"That's no lady; that's a feller"*.

It was about this time (1964/68) that we had a Dutch buyer who used to write us charming letters. He had obviously decided that the British were a sporting nation and accordingly would address us in apparently colloquial English. I have two such letters before me as I write, and I quote: *"The lots were not up to the surprise I expected, but next time better, said the burglar who went to prison for the fifth time. Please add the cost to your next shot at my birds"*. Also, *"If you have the opportunity to put up more Dutch lots, you will find me in pursuit of the fox"*.

Over the years the collections we have handled often contained evidence of extra-mural activities. On three occasions we encountered considerable amounts of pornographic material, one such lot having been acquired by the vendor, a pillar of his local church.

Once we found a quantity of torrid correspondence from the vendor's mistress in a nearby town - to which he had attached copies of his equally thoughtful replies! The disposal of such material had to be done with obvious sensitivity, usually by fire, especially if the vendor's widow was still alive.

Turning to eccentrics on the other side of the counter, I remember one dealer who used to attend our early sales in Leeds. He had an old established stamp shop in that city which he had inherited from his father. He would arrive at the sale armed with some scales. He told me that he always purchased stamp collections by weight.

I cannot remember him ever succeeding in purchasing a lot, and in the circumstances this is hardly surprising. It is of course the usual practice to buy kiloware and on-paper mixtures by weight. He was, however, interested in buying collections in albums. He would not inspect the contents but would solemnly place the albums on his scales.

I don't know what yardstick he used for valuation, but he would tell me that the lots were all over-valued. Eventually he tired of coming to the sales, and I was told that the business had closed down.

Of course some of us are blessed with the occasional eccentric relative as well. We had an aunt in the family who was quite potty, but who was much loved by her numerous nephews and nieces for her very oddness. She would send us all cards on birthdays and at Christmas. Each would be endorsed "wonderful present to follow" – they never did! She also had a passion for hats although she seldom wore one. When she died my cousin found over 400 hats of various styles and vintages at her home. He presented them to his Church – he also was somewhat of an eccentric. I'm sure they were most grateful!

A few months ago I observed a very much worse for wear car proceeding slowly down London Road not far from our offices. Both front and rear wings were battered and the bumpers were a sad sight. Several running repairs had been effected with Sellotape including two cracked windows. The driver was a hairy, bearded bookish type, and as far as I could tell of late middle age. That he had an indeed necessary sense of humour was obvious, because on the rear, as yet unbroken, window hung a notice "ERRARE HUMANUS EST". Ah, I thought, a Latin scholar – and no doubt a stamp collector to boot.

My memory of this incident was revived recently when I read in the Telegraph Arts and Books Supplement a review of "Latin: or the Empire of a Sign" by Francoise Waquet, published by Verso at £20. Basically the book is the final epitaph for a long dead language. Like so many of my generation who suffered having to decide the declension of umpteen Latin nouns, I always wondered what on earth the language would do for me in later life. It would surely only be useful if your chosen career was to teach it! I believe that in the old days doctors always wrote their prescriptions in Latin, but today a doctor's handwriting is equally incomprehensible. Actually I became passably useful at Latin. This was a good thing because 65 years ago the School Certificate examination allowed a credit in Latin to offset a fail in maths – a subject which still remains a mystery to me.

Try as I may I cannot remember anything of the language except perhaps "Nauta cottam habet" – the sailor having a cottage being a most useful phrase in the Elementa Latina. I seem to remember that Caesar was forever advancing strongly into hither Gaul and later in Virgil quite enjoying the games which were considerably more blood-thirsty than today's versions. I do remember small boys wishing to dispose of some unwanted trifle would cry "quis", and the resulting reply of "ego" – and of course you can always demonstrate your scholarship and excuse any error of fact or judgement with "ERRARE HUMANUS EST".

**With my first wife Mary
at Congress, 1987.**

**Presenting one of the Congress Medals
to John Sussex, 1987.**

Our 200th Sale was advertised in *"Stamp Collecting"* **1969**

Chronological List of Cavendish's Business Addresses, 1952-2002

1952-1967	Derby Stamp Shop, Curzon Street, Derby.
1967-1978	Cavendish Auction Rooms, 69 The Wardwick, Derby.
1979-1995	Cavendish Auction Rooms, Progressive Building, Sitwell Street, Derby DE1 2JP.
1995-2002	Cavendish House, 153-157 London Road, Derby DE1 2SY.

CHAPTER 5

Still Going Strong

I can look back on over 60 years "in stamps" from 1947 when my small enterprise started in Derby. It does of course go back further than that as I started collecting in a spasmodic fashion when stamp collecting was the major hobby with school boys. All the boys' magazines carried dealers' advertisements for "approvals" with the added incentives of "free gifts". Every town of any size could boast at least one stamp shop and the "boy trade" could usually be relied upon to pay the rent and rates. Now a stamp shop is quite a rarity mainly owing to high rentals and the majority of dealers operate postally from home or office or take stalls at stamp fairs, which are themselves a fairly recent departure.

For many years the stamp auction houses had been the preserve of a handful of firms, mainly in London. This has changed since the war and several other auctioneers have entered the field. In the Midlands we were pioneers in this respect. At one time the main buyers at auction were the trade. This has all changed and most serious collectors now buy at auction. The publication of estimated prices, virtually unknown pre-war, has helped this trend.

A comparatively recent phenomenon is the so-called "Postal Auction" - a misnomer of course; they should be termed "Sales by tender". They do nevertheless enjoy considerable popularity. Collecting habits have changed. The postal historian has emerged and surely takes pride of place over the mere stamp collector, but equal in status to the philatelist. My own view is that both stamps and postal history can happily co-exist in the same collection. The one enhances the other, and that is how I get enjoyment from my own collection.

The question so often asked, mainly by non-collectors, is whether the hobby we enjoy is, in fact, dying. The answer is yes and no. If sheer numbers is the criterion the answer must be 'yes'. The membership of philatelic societies generally has fallen over the last thirty or so years. The average school boy no longer collects - television and pop records are but two competing enemies. On the other hand auction realisations continue to rise. The exhibits at major exhibitions continue to improve and would-be exhibitors have to work hard for acceptance. On the whole I think the future of the hobby is certainly safe in the short term, and probably for several decades.

James G-T, Francis Kiddle (at that time President of the Royal Philatelic Society), and myself at the opening of Cavendish House, 1995.

I am frequently asked by non-collectors if stamps are a good investment. The answer is, of course, also yes and no! The long term collector who is discriminating in his purchases, probably specialising to some degree, and including items of postal history to illustrate the subject, will usually be very gratified with the result when the time comes to sell - or his heirs will be amazed at the proceeds of the sale of dad's old stamp collection!

However, the punter who sets out to buy purely for investment will invariably come unstuck. Even the most astute businessman can make the most elementary mistakes when buying solely for profit. Such a gentleman regularly attended our sales in Manchester during the late sixties and early seventies. He was a wholesale importer of textile goods and clearly had ample funds at his disposal. His purchases were usually early to modern G.B. high values and he was right in assuming that in due course this material would increase in value. He telephoned me one day and asked me, with some urgency, to come over to his home in Wilmslow. On my arrival he asked for my opinion if he were to corner the entire post office stock of the then current 1967 British Painting issue. When I said this would be a disaster he looked shocked and said that he had started to do just that. He then led me into his study and there was the entire stock held at the Edinburgh P.O. Philatelic Bureau which had cost him over £39,000. No doubt the Bureau was already in the process of replacing the stock from central stores and Harrisons warned to stand-by to make another printing! Eventually the stamps were sold at a considerate discount to a mail-order trading house.

Towards the end of the 1970s and in the early 1980s there was a boom in stamps, fuelled by newspaper articles and ever increasing auction realisations - indeed on one occasion we sold an unmounted mint 1929 £1 P.U.C. for £1,400! After the sale the vendor, a local collector, came up to me and said *"I hardly dare tell you this, Mr. Manton, but you sold me that stamp for £7 in 1950!"*

This rapidly rising market spawned a rash of "Investment Advisors" and advertisements tipping the purchase of various sets and single stamps. So-called "Investment Portfolios" were offered for sale by philatelic spivs, composed mainly of poor quality and overpriced stamps. However, a number of well-known stamp firms marketed "Investment Portfolios", the contents of which were of quite reasonable quality but being priced at the then current enhanced retail prices they could never possibly rank as an "investment". In subsequent years we have been called upon to sell scores of these lots and frequently have had the task of explaining to the vendor that the lot is unlikely to make half or even a third of the original purchase price!

One friend of mine who is a dedicated investor on the Stock Exchange asked me to make him up an investment lot for about £10,000 and was very pained when I declined. He was only partially satisfied when I explained that I wanted to retain his friendship.

I have joined the 21 CLUB - meaning that I was born in 1921. Being 80 there is no noticeable difference. The stiffening of the joints and the shortage of breath have been a gradual process. There was a time when I could - and did - run the three-quarters of a mile up from Matlock to my home on the hillside overlooking the town. Now I walk sedately with frequent stops to admire the view - or take a taxi which seems a much more sensible thing to do. I am a great believer in the advice - when you feel like exercise, lie down until the feeling passes.

The memory is certainly not so good. For events which occurred many years ago it is still quite keen, hence these recollections, but recent happenings have a tendency to "slip the mind". However I am assured that this is a common failing. I enjoy reading all the military obituaries in the *Daily Telegraph* and observe that most of the departed were in their late 70s or early 80s. This is in no way done in a spirit of self-flagellation because I have every intention of being around for some time yet - after all my father made 98 and was in good form until the end!

On the actual day I enjoyed my 80th Birthday Lunch which involved my two families, except for the American end, together with one great-grand-daughter and a few close friends. The previous week we held a Luncheon Party for early and current members of Cavendish Auctions together with their various spouses. It was a happy day and 38 were able to attend. The company was in its 50th year and Pam and I were able to welcome several who were with us almost from the start - notably Sheila Kimber and Geoffrey Whitehead who both did so much to give Cavendish the reputation it enjoys today.

This is being written a few days into the New Year 2001. Several days during the Christmas period have been spent in the Cotswolds with my son and daughter-in-law. 'Mick' has pretension as a connoisseur of wine and I am gradually recovering from intensive and varied libations - not that I found the treatment at all unwelcome. Grandsons and their wives made periodic appearances, one accompanied by great-grand-daughter, and the other back from honeymoon on Christmas Eve.

Not all the time was spent partying, and midnight on Christmas Eve at the Church of the Holy Cross at Avening was indeed a memorable occasion. This splendid 10th or 11th century church was packed with worshippers and illuminated by hundreds of candles.

The snow arrived a few days later and the drive back to Matlock was fraught at times. We thought that a dinner party we had arranged for the following night would have to be cancelled, but in the event most of our guests were able to arrive. It proved to be a very late night which was bad staff work really because I was shooting the next day. Any pheasants which came near me were pretty safe!

In the circumstances we were happy to spend a quiet New Year's Eve at home with a light supper and a good bottle of claret. At midnight we watched from our windows the many rockets going up from parties in the valley below.

Of course very little of this has much to do with stamps – but does it matter?

A roomful of buyers watch me receive bids for Lot 1 at our 500th auction in September 1995.

Appendix

Extracts from Cavendish's very first auction catalogue, January 1952.

CONDITIONS OF SALE

1. The highest bidder to be deemed the purchaser. Should any dispute arise the lot(s) to be re-offered at the discretion of the Auctioneer.

2. The purchaser to give name and place of abode, and to pay a deposit if required. All lots to be cleared at the conclusion of the Sale and the purchase money paid in full. In the case of Postal Buyers, lots purchased must be paid for within three days of receipt of advice.

3. The advance in bidding to be regulated at the Auctioneer's discretion.

4. The Auctioneer reserves the right to bid on behalf of vendors and buyers unable to attend the Sale personally.

5. Each lot is sold as genuine and accurately described, but in the event of misdescription, Postal Buyers are entitled to take or reject providing that notice of such rejection be made and the lot returned within seven days from the date of sale. This guarantee does not apply in the case of collections or mixed lots.

6. Upon failure to comply with the above conditions any uncleared lots may be resold by public or private sale and the deficiency (if any) shall be made good by the defaulter, together with any incidental charges.

NOTICE TO VENDORS

LOTS CAN NOW BE ACCEPTED FOR FUTURE SALES. Suitable material for disposal by Auction would include good sets and single varieties, single-country and general collections, Club books and mixed lots, proofs, essays etc. Always REGISTER ALL LOTS.

COMMISSION 12½% : Minimum per lot 2/6

Lots failing to reach the reserve price will be charged at the rate of 2/6 per lot. All lots are considered to have been received by us for UNRESERVED SALE unless definite written regarding disposal are received by us at least three days prior to Sale.

THIS CATALOGUE IS FOR THE DERBY SALE

Sales to follow are

SHEFFIELD 14th March, 7.00p.m. at The Grand Hotel.
DONCASTER in April, date and venue to be fixed.

The charge for Catalogues is 6d. each, or 2/6 will ensure that you receive all catalogues issued during 1952.

Correspondence to : 75, Saltergate, Chesterfield. Tel 2980 Ext Stamps.
Matters requiring the urgent attention of Mr Manton should be addressed to Wardwick Chambers, 69, The Wardwick, Derby.

VIEWING OF LOTS

Lots may be viewed at 75, Saltergate, Chesterfield on Tuesday 15th Jan, from 10am to 4pm.
also
In the Saleroom at the Railway Institute, Derby, on the day of the sale from 3pm to 6.30.

LOT NUMBER	DESCRIPTION	ESTIMATED VALUE	No. of Stamps
1.	General Collection in Lincoln Album.	52/6	2085
2.	Collection in Mercury Album	22/6	abt 650
3.	Collection of Colonials and Foreign in Strand Album	£3	2376
4.	General Collection in Mercury Album	30/-	1289
5.	Colonial and Foreign collection in Quickchange Album	50/-	1344
6.	B.Col Collection on loose-leaves. Nice clean lot. Many mintsets.	85/-	1069
7.	Small Stockbook containing assortment Colonial and Foreign. Nice lot.	£3	abt1200
8.	Club Book contg used GeoVI including 9 Barbados 8d. obsolete.	18/-	51
9.	The good selection of Colonials. Mostly mint inc S.W.A. Silver Jub. comp mint, useful Malaya, Iraq, Zanzibar etc.	90/-	abt150

Page 2

LOT NUMBER	DESCRIPTION	ESTIMATED VALUE	No. of Stamps
10.	Interesting selection of Covers, mostly GERMAN. Some good stamps.	40/-	Covrs 57
11.	Cardboard Box containing good-class Colonial and Foreign Office Mixture on paper. Mostly pictorials and commems.	£3	abt 1400
12.	Cardboard Box contg mainly line-eng G.B. and a few covers.	35/-	quantit
13.	Sel Mint G.B. in pocket folder including £1 Silver Wedding.	£2	64
14.	Sel Mint Br Cols in tin box. Face over £3.	50/-	Qty
15.	Sel Mint Foreign in pocket book. Stated to Cat over 130/-	25/-	Qty
16.	Bundle B.Col Club Sheet remainders. Priced to over £7.	35/-	Qty
17.	Bundle of Foreign ditto. Priced to over £15.	55/-	Qty
18.	Goddens New Ideal VolII, almost as new.		Album
19.	do Vol III, in similar condition.		Album
20.	Goddens Graduate Album, as new.		Album
21.	Gibbons Swing-O-Ring, as new.		Album
22.	Gibbons Catalogues Parts 4 & 5		Catalogue
23.	Collection of Coronations on First Day Covers	75/-	
24.	a similar lot, but mounted in folder	75/-	
SILVER JUBILEES			
25.	Antigua Mint Set	17/6	4
26.	British Honduras Mint Set	9/-	4
27.	Cayman Islands Fine Used Set	12/6	4
28.	Cook Islands Mint Set	8/-	3
29.	Grenada Mint Set	12/6	4
30.	Kenya,Uganda & Tanganyika Mint Set	8/-	4
31.	Leeward Is Fine Used Set	15/-	4
32.	St Kitts Mint Set	11/-	4
33.	St Lucia Mint Set	17/6	4
34.	S. Rhodesia and Swaziland Mint Sets	13/-	8
35.	Swaziland Mint Set	6/-	4
36.	Trinidad & Tobago Mint Set	10/-	4
37.	Turks & Caicos Mint Set	9/-	4
38.	Virgin Is Mint Set	11/-	4
SILVER WEDDINGS			
39.	Bahamas Mint Set	40/-	2
40.	Barbados, Leeward Is, Montserrat Mint Sets	21/-	6
41.	Bermuda Mint Set	35/-	2
42.	British Honduras Mint Set	77/6	2
43.	Cayman Islands Mint Set	15/-	2
44.	Grenada Mint Set	18/-	2
45.	Turks & Caicos Is Mint Set	17/6	2
U.P.U.			
46.	Aden and States Comp Mint Cat 68/6		12
47.	a similar lot		12
48.	Malaya 7 diff sets all mint Cat 52/6		28
49.	Seychelles Mint Set		4

LOT NUMBER	DESCRIPTION	ESTIMATED VAL.	No of Stamps
155.	GERMAN STATES. BAVARIA. The Mint and used collect ion on slip-in card. Cat £4.12.6.		135
156.	do HAMBURG & Hanover. Useful Lot. Many good stamps. Cat £46.	£7.15.	26
157.	GREAT BRITAIN 1840. 2d. Mulready Wrapper. Unused, slightly soiled.	20/-	1
158.	do 1840 1d. Black Pl 3, on cover dated 28th May 40. Fair.	32/6	1
159.	do 1d. Black Lettered JA. Red MC. Fine on cover.	30/-	1
160.	do 1d. Black do JB. Deep Red MC. Four margins on cov.	35/-	1
161.	do 1d. Black. Pl 1b. Vertical pair, one cut o'wise fine.		2
162.	do 1d. Black, possibly large JC of Pl 1b. Three margin copy.		1
163.	do 1d. Black, four margins, app unused but sold as is.		1
164.	do 1d. Black. Red MC, guide line, fine just touched at bottom.		1
165.	do 1d. Black. Red MC, lettered LF, trace of blueing. Fair.		1
166.	do 1d. Black. Fine four margins, lettered GI. Worn plate.	30/-	1
167.	do 1d. Black. Pl 7 re-entry. App unused or cleaned?		1
168.	do 1d. Black. Pl 7, lettered AB, Red MC. Fine.	27/6	1
169.	do 1d. Black. Pl. 8, Black MC. Four margin copy.		1
170.	do 1d. Black. Pl 9, guide line, Red MC, close one side.		1
171.	do 2d. Blue. Very fine, four margins, black MC	75/-	1
172.	do 2d. Blue. Fine pair, red MC. One stamp has slight crease.	65/-	2
173.	do 2d. Blue. Fair copy, not cut into. Black MC.	25/-	1
174.	do 2d. Blue, also ditto 1841, both with defects.	15/-	2
175.	do The collection of line-engraved on Windsor leaves. Inc 1d. Black, 2d. Blue, later imperfs, 1854 issues a good range, 1d. plates complete ex two, 2d. plates comp, ½d. plates comp (inc some mint), 1½d plates. High Cat value.	£5-£6.	229
176.	do 1854-1857. The interesting collection. Stated to Cat over £34.	95/-	70
177.	do 1841 1d. Red in block of 6, small defects and scarce thus and of fine app. Also 2d.Blue, a fine strip of 3.	47/6	9
178.	do 1841 1d. Red. Inverted S. Fine four margin copy. Cat 70/-	30/-	1
179.	do 1841 2d. Blue. App unused with guide line. Three margin copy.	15/-	1
180.	do 1d. Rose red, Plate No 212, mint block of eight.	25/-	8
181.	do 1858-64 2d. Blue. Part reconstructed Pl 14. Cat £20.16.0.	35/-	64
182.	do do do Pl 15. Cat £23.8.0.	40/-	72
183.	do 1855-73. The surface printed issues on Windsor leaves. High catalogue value. Condition poor to fine.	60/-	53
184.	do 1855 Surface prints d. S.G.Nos 62, 64, 66, 67, and 68. The Fine selection. Cat £11.12. 6.	65/-	5
185.	do 1873. 2½d. Rosy-mauve, the collection, fair to fine. Cat over£13.	42/6	18
186.	do 1873/83. Collection of surface printed on Windsor leaves, inc high values. Very high cat value. Cond poor to fine.	80/-	72
187.	do 1883. 2/6 on blued (175). Nice used copy. Cat 90/-	37/6	1
188.	do a similar lot, but with B.P.A. Certificate		1
189.	do 1887 3d. Deep purple on orange, nice used on piece. Cat 50/-	16/-	1
190.	do Ed VII 5/- S.G.265. Mint Cat 65/-	35/-	1

LOT NUMBER	DESCRIPTION	ESTIMATED VALUE	No of STAMPS
191.	GREAT BRITAIN Ed VII 10/- S.G.265 Superb Used Cat £3	30/-	1
192.	do Ed VII £1 S.G.266 Fine Used Cat £6	£3	1
193.	do Ed VII 5/- S.G.318 Fine used pair. Cat 40/-	22/6	2
194.	do Ed VII £1 S.G.320 Superb used Ca$ £5.	55/-	1
195.	do 1912-22 1½d. PeneY Error (364a) Mint	35/-	1
196.	do 1913 £1 green. Avery nice used and well-centred copy. Cat £14.	£7	1
197.	do 1925 Wembley Exhibition. Mint corner blocks of 4. Cat 105/-	50/-	8
198.	do 1940 Postal Centy, mint set in blocks of four.		24
199.	do Quantity embossed Telegraph forms. Ed VII & Geo VI. All unused.		Qty
200.	GRENADA. THE MAINLY MINT COLLECTION TO 1934. GOOD RANGE OF QUEENS AND USEFUL EDWARDS AND GEORGES. CAT NEARLY £48.	£16	84
201.	do S.G. 100a Cat 30/- Mint.	14/-	1
202.	do S.G. 101 Cat 70/- Mint.	40/-	1
203.	do 1938 10/- (163) A superb used Block of four. Cat £11	£6	4
204.	HONG KONG. Selection of Geo V to 1 dollar, all used.		20
205.	do 1941 Centenary set used.		5
206.	INDIA. The useful mint and used collection. Mainly early issues and Georges with vals to 25Rs. Stated to Cat over £45.	£6	133
207.	do 1854. ½ anna Blue. The very fine, large margined copies, various Dies. Stated to Cat £18.15.0.	£6	5
208.	do 1854 4 As. Fine proof on thin paper.	45/-	1
209.	do S.G.515, fine used. Cat £8.	35/-	1
210.	do Heavily duplicated coll in Paragon album. A useful lot.		100's
211.	IRAQ. 1931 Set complete mint (ex ½a) Cat 86/7.	35/-	11
212.	do 1931 THE RARE 25rs VIOLET, SUPERB MINT. CAT £25.	£13	1
213.	do 1932 Provisionals. Mint set to 200 fils. Cat 63/1.	27/6	14
214.	do S.G. 075 Mint Cat 35/-	15/-	1
215.	ITALY & STATES. The interesting coll mainly used. Stated to Cat £14	45/-	192
216.	JAMAICA. S.G.102a Part gum and small thin.	5/-	1
217.	JAPAN. The mint and used coll of mainly earlies. Stated to cat £27.	45/-	95
218.	JUGO-SLAVIA. Small coll with many useful items. Cat about £5.	23/-	195
219.	KENYA, UGANDA & TANGANYIKA. S.G.26 foll by a selection of Georges, Mainly mint. Cat £9.	55/-	15
220.	do 1935 Set Mint to 2/-.	15/-	10
221.	KOREA. Coll inc earlies and 1903 issue comp. Cat £4.	35/-	18
222.	LABUAN. 1902/03 set Mint.	7/6	12
223.	LEEWARD IS. The mainly mint collection with good range of Queens, Edwards to 2/6 and Georges to 5/-. Cat £20.9.1.	£3	69
224.	do S.G.8 Mint Cat 70/-	37/6	1
225.	LUXEMBURG. The very useful lot. Strong in earlies. High Cat value.	£3	100's
226.	MALAYA - JOHORE 1896 S.G.35 to40, also the error S.G. 47. Cat 46/3	21/-	7
227.	do PAHANG S.G. 40, 41, and 42. All Mint.	30/-	3
228.	MALTA. S.G.153 Mint Cat 50/-	22/6	1

Index of People & Philatelic Organisations